THE MEDICAL ADVISER

IN

LIFE ASSURANCE.

THE

MEDICAL ADVISER

IN

LIFE ASSURANCE

BY

EDWARD HENRY SIEVEKING, M.D.,

FELLOW OF THE ROYAL COLLEGE OF PHYSICIANS,
PHYSICIAN TO ST. MARY'S AND THE LOCK HOSPITALS, PHYSICIAN
EXTRAORDINARY TO THE QUEEN, PHYSICIAN IN ORDINARY
TO THE PRINCE OF WALES, ETC.

HARTFORD, CONN
N. P. FLETCHER & CO
1875

PREFACE.

EVERY medical man, in the course of his professional career, is now-a-days more or less frequently brought into contact with insurance business, and questions are submitted to him in connection with life policies, the answers to which often demand a special kind of knowledge not always to be found in the ordinary handbooks of medicine, nor suggested by the clinical study of disease. The information required is partly empirical, partly scattered about in a variety of works, generally the Transactions of Societies, and similar publications, not readily accessible to the busy practitioner. It is the object of the following pages to collect and place before the reader, in a concise and easily available form, such facts and figures as appear to be required by the physician, to enable him to arrive at a correct estimate of the many interesting contingencies upon which life insurance business rests. Great as have been the strides made by students of medicine of late years, much yet remains to be done before we can claim for medicine all the exactness which belongs to true science; and in few departments is the absence of precision more felt than in the range of topics which are summed up under the term of the expectation of life of the individual.

It is hoped that the present essay may assist in defining what is actually known on this important subject; and that while it may afford aid to some in determining questions of great social significance, it may encourage others to publish the results of their studies of vital statistics, and of their experience upon particular points bearing upon life insurance.

I have been careful to give every writer from whom I have drawn information his due, and, for the benefit of my readers, have been particular in referring them to the sources from which my knowledge has been gathered. I have great pleasure in expressing the obligations I am under to my predecessors in this department of social science; and also to my friend Mr. John Messent, for assistance he has rendered me by advice upon some actuarial questions, and by the loan of various works not to be found in medical libraries. I am especially indebted to him for some passages contained in the last chapter, in which the medico-legal aspects of life insurance are discussed.

E. H. S.

17 MANCHESTER SQUARE, LONDON,
December 1873.

CONTENTS.

CHAPTER VII.

CHAPTER VII.

CHAPTER I.

INTRODUCTION.

AMONG the features that may be regarded as characteristic of modern Christian society, Life Insurance stands prominently forward as peculiarly unselfish. Its main object, provision for those whom death deprives of their bread-winner and protector, entails self-denial and forethought on the part of the individual who takes out a policy, and may thus become indirectly a boon to himself, by compelling thrift, and keeping alive the best feelings of our common humanity. The more the principles of Life Insurance are understood, the more certain are they to be appreciated and acted upon; and while they give to society a guarantee for the uprightness and honesty of the individual, he in return assists in rendering more firm and stable the very groundwork of the republic. The relative number of inhabitants of different localities who have taken out policies of life insurance may not inappropriately be regarded as an index of the prosperity of the communities they belong to, for they afford direct evidence of the existence of those qualities, thrift, forethought and consideration for others, upon which our social comfort and happiness chiefly depend. Those qualities do not necessarily bear a direct ratio to the amount of rateable property possessed by these different communities, but they form the essential basis of Christian society.

But Life Insurance, like all human enterprises, requires to be carried on with care and caution. An abstract good may be capable of abuse, and so unfortunately life insurance has occasionally been turned to a bad account. Direct fraud has crept in, of which instructive examples may be found in the literature of the subject;* but carelessness and a neglect of rules, that must guide all commercial transactions, have had more to do with the failure of insurance enterprises than attempts at deception, which are guarded against with comparative facility. Life insurance is essentially a commercial contract between two parties; the basis of which is, on the one hand, the truthful representation of certain data on the part of the insuree, and the undertaking on the part of the insurer to pay a covenanted sum of money, provided the former has duly fulfilled his part of the agreement, on the occurrence of certain contingencies. Now all insurance tables are calculated so as to allow a margin of profit to the companies, provided that the mortality does not exceed a certain ratio. An insurance company cannot conduct a safe business unless it is able to restrict its mortality within the rate provided, and to defray its expenses out of this margin allowed

* The reader is specially referred to Annals, Anecdotes, and Legends, a Chronicle of Life Insurance, by John Francis: London, 1853; and The Insurance Guide and Handbook, by C. Walford: London, 1867. Second edition. The latter is a mine of valuable and trustworthy information, and we shall have frequent occasion to quote from it.

for that purpose, in the absence of exceptional sources of profit. It is therefore in the interest of all policyholders, both for their security and profit, that the company should use every reasonable precaution to see that the basis of the contract on the part of the insuree is unimpeachable, just as it is the interest of the latter to ascertain that the company with which he proposes to insure will at any time be able to fulfil its share of the contract and pay the claim when it falls due.

The misfortunes which have overtaken some companies, especially of late years, have suggested the desirability of converting them all into Government property, a process which has not met with much support; but the greater control exercised under the Act of 1870 has been hailed with satisfaction, although it has entailed much labour upon them, by all well-established and respectable companies, because it is believed that it will prevent the formation of bubble undertakings, and give the public as great a guarantee of good behaviour on behalf of those existing, or to exist in future, as can fairly be expected.

The real stability of an insurance company*

* We follow the prevailing custom of employing the terms insurance and assurance interchangeably, *pace* Mr. Babbage, who defined *Assurance* as a contract dependent upon the duration of life, which must either happen or fail; *Insurance* as a contract relating to any other uncertain event which may partly happen or partly fail; thus in adjusting the price for insurance of houses and ships, regard is always had to the chance of salvage arising from partial destruction.—(Walford, p. 2.)

must after all depend upon the manner and character of the work done, and it is only in so far as to afford the general public an easy means of ascertaining that the staff of the companies are honestly and conscientiously doing the work intrusted to them, that Government control is either wise or desirable. The whole science of insurance has been developed by individual effort, and it would be indeed strange if pecuniary interests, involving nearly one hundred million sterling,* and second only in their magnitude to the railway interests of the

* The reader may be interested in the following statistics regarding English life insurance business. There were at the end of 1871, 106 returns filed to the Board of Trade (three foreign institutions being omitted and two incomplete returns) with the following results:—

Income.

Total premiums	£9,743,600	5	0½
Consideration for Annuities granted .	254,133	1	6¾
Interest and Dividend	4,040,175	3	8½
Miscellaneous Receipts	115,511	1	1
	£14,153,419	11	4¾

Disbursements.

Claims	£8,200,993	1	2½
Surrendered Cash Bonuses and returned Premiums	1,063,087	6	8½
Annuities	386,867	0	5
Expenses (including Dividends to Shareholders)	1,870,392	4	7¾
Miscellaneous	106,771	17	6
	£11,628,111	10	5¾
The Assets amounting in the aggregate to	£92,332,222	14	3½

country, interests that have enjoyed no Government patronage during their minority, should now, when they have attained the stature of vigorous manhood, require to be put under a nurse's care like the rickety bantling of sickly parents.

The seed of the plant that has grown to such dimensions was sown in very modern times; in fact no data upon which any plan of the kind could have been formed existed, until that national self-knowledge, which depends upon vital and mortuary statistics, had been cultivated. Parish registers were not kept in England till 1538; but it was not till nearly two centuries later that they were rendered available for calculations on the value and duration of life by the addition of the ages of the dead. "The earliest movement in economical arithmetic, and the closest approximation to the data on which life assurance is founded," was made by John Graunt in the beginning of the seventeenth century, in his work entitled, "Natural and Political Observations on the Bills of Mortality." Mr. Walford, who gives a detailed history of the growth of life insurance, tells us that many of Graunt's observations are as curious for their accuracy as for their originality. As a specimen of the curious suggestions which he makes, which may be of use to modern political economists, he advised, when the entire population of London was about 384,000, that means should be taken to check the growth of the town, the first point to attend to being, to ascertain whether the city of London had "grown big enough."

It is unnecessary for our purpose to dwell on the

details of the development of life insurance business. Suffice it to say that the first actual insurance company was established in 1714; the Union Assurance Society, the London Assurance Corporation, and the Royal Exchange Assurance Corporation, followed, in 1720; the Equitable was founded in 1762; the Pelican in 1797. At the present moment the Insurance Directory gives the names of 152 companies transacting life insurance business, showing the enormous extension which this branch of providential commerce has taken. Whether it be desirable that a larger number of companies should be called into existence is a moot point. There are now a sufficient number to insure healthy competition; and as at present only a small proportion of the entire community are insured, both the security of the existing companies and the advantage of the insurees would be probably best consulted by the latter rallying round the old flags, rather than by setting up new standards, and involving themselves in all the trouble, risk, and expense, attending the creation of new companies. Fire insurance dates a little further back than life insurance. The "Hand in Hand," which, at a later period, also charged itself with life business, took its origin at the end of the seventeenth century, having been founded in the year 1696, under the designation of "The Amicable Contribution," which it soon after changed for that of the well-known association still transacting insurance business under both forms in Blackfriars.* Grateful as we

*No history of English men and manners would be complete without a delineation of the phases through which

must feel to the enterprising men who first promoted honest life insurance business, we imply no censure when we say that, as a matter of fact, they were groping in the dark, as they could possess no definite principle to guide them, until it was possible to establish a firm basis by the preparation of reliable mortality tables. Their rates * were extravagantly

insurance business has passed. In the early part of the last century John Bull rode this particular hobby until he appeared to have lost his wits. Fortunately the disease did not prove incurable; and, after wandering about in a state of maniacal aberration for a time, the patient recovered without permanent damage to his constitutional vigour. Insurances against thieves, housebreakers, and highwaymen, for making pasteboard, for making boards out of sawdust, against lying, against death from drinking Geneva, against divorces, for the preservation of female chastity, were some of the many peculiar objects for which companies were established. But fire and life bore the palm over all competitors; and their advocates appear to have shown much pertinacity of purpose, to the discomfiture of some quiet people. The following lines, quoted by Walford from the *New Monthly Magazine* of a later date, illustrate this phase, and perhaps also give the correct clue to the original meaning of the terms which Babbage has otherwise defined:—

"By fire and life insurers next
I'm intercepted, pester'd, vex'd,
Almost beyond endurance;
And though the schemes appear unsound,
Their advocates are seldom found
Deficient in assurance."

* The early offices charged enormous premiums, from not possessing reliable data for calculation. The premium to assure £100 for one year, on the life of any age between 12 and 45, was as much as £5; whereas the assurance for the whole life on the same amount now ranges, according to age, from £1 : 8s, to £3 : 12s.

high, a fault that might even now be considered as leaning to virtue's side, since it added to the security of the policyholders, by increasing the assets of the companies. To a Unitarian preacher, Dr. Price, belongs the honour of having elaborated the first English mortality tables, which, from his having employed the registers of the births and deaths of the town of Northampton for his calculations, have received the name, and are still known as, the Northampton Mortality Tables. They were published in 1780, and were especially constructed for the use of the old Equitable Society. Dr. Halley had, at an earlier date, from the mortality records of the town of Breslau, drawn up tables giving the probabilities of life at every age; but, from being buried in the Philosophical Transactions (1693), they bore no fruit; and it was reserved to a recent date to disinter them, and to accord to their author the distinguished merit that belongs to him. Nearly forty years elapsed from the appearance of Dr. Price's tables, before the Carlisle Tables of Mortality were constructed, by Mr. Milne, from observations furnished by Dr. Heysham upon the registers of Carlisle. There is sufficient agreement in the results yielded by Mr. Milne, and Dr. Price's calculations to establish their general trustworthiness; but, during the interval that elapsed between their publication, actuarial science had received ampler development; and the greater precision and lower mortality demonstrated by Mr. Milne justly established the pre-eminence of the Carlisle Tables, from the date of their publication, in 1816. They continue to form the basis upon which premiums of insurance are calculated at the present day.

The main object of all insurance tables is to demonstrate the average expectation of life, as deducible from the mortuary registers of the country for the entire population. No one has probably done more during the present generation to advance our knowledge in this branch of statistical science than Dr. Farr, of the Registrar-General's office, aided, as he has been, by active workers distributed all over the country. Nor have their labours been confined to determining the general expectation of life at different ages of the members of the community at large, but Dr. Farr, Mr. Willich, Dr. Guy, Dr. Taylor, Mr. Neison, Mr. Scratchley, and many others, have worked out the problems of the duration of life in separate classes and trades with a minuteness that leaves nothing to be desired. We shall take a future opportunity of availing ourselves of the practical results they have attained in connection with various questions of detail; but it is ever to be borne in mind that, however valuable and true general averages are, they cannot be held as establishing the expectation of the individual, in whom many contingencies have to be considered before we determine the exact position he occupies towards the general average. It is for the purpose of ascertaining this position, and estimating the bearing of the accidents of hereditary influence, personal constitution, of trade and occupation, and of previous acquired taints or morbid influences, than the physician, possessing special qualifications for analysing these various elements, must be called in to assist the actuary. While the latter deals with large numbers and averages, the former is more trained to observe individuals, and to watch exceptional cases; the objects of life insurance will be in good case where the two understand one another, and seek heartily to co-operate to the same end. This is well illustrated by the remark of Mr. Babbage, when he says that "nothing is more uncertain than the duration of life when the maxim is applied to the individual; but there are few things less subject to fluctuation than the duration of human life in a multitude of individuals." As the question of the expectation of life underlies all insurance calculations, and affects largely the estimate of the individual insuree by the medical officer, we give the following tables here, in which the expectation of life or the period an individual may expect to live, according to the observations made in England, on the Continent of Europe, and in the United States of America, is shown :—

TABLE I.—Showing the Expectation of Life, or the period an individual of a given age may be expected to live, according to the following Tables of Mortality, deduced from Observations made in England.*

Completed Age.	Carlisle.	Northampton.	Seventeen Life Offices, 1843.	Government Annuitants.		Completed Age.
				Males.	Females.	
0	38.72	25.18	....	50.16	55.51	0
1	44.68	32.74	....	50.13	55.59	1
5	51.25	40.84	....	48.93	54.23	5
10	48.82	39.78	....	45.57	51.05	10
13	46.51	37.83	....	43.31	48.70	13
15	45.00	36.51	....	41.76	47.19	15
17	43.57	35.20	....	40.29	45.86	17
20	41.46	33.43	41.49	38.39	43.99	20
23	39.31	31.88	39.39	36.87	42.09	23
25	37.86	30.85	37.98	35.90	40.81	25
27	36.41	29.82	36.56	34.86	39.52	27
30	34.34	28.27	34.43	33.17	37.57	30
33	32.3[illegible]	26.72	32.30	31.40	35.61	33
35	31.00	25.68	30.87	30.17	34.31	35
37	29.64	24.64	29.44	28.91	33.04	37
40	27.61	23.08	27.28	27.02	31.12	40
43	25.71	21.54	25.12	25.08	29.14	43
45	24.46	20.52	23.69	23.75	27.81	45
47	23.17	19.51	22.27	22.38	26.44	47
49	21.81	18.49	20.87	20.98	25.06	49
50	21.11	17.99	20.18	20.30	24.35	50
51	20.39	17.50	19.50	19.62	23.65	51
53	18.97	16.54	18.16	18.34	22.22	53
55	17.58	15.58	16.86	17.15	20.79	55
57	16.21	14.63	15.59	16.02	19.38	57
59	14.92	13.68	14.37	14.93	18.00	59
60	14.34	13.21	13.77	14.39	17.35	60
61	13.82	12.75	13.18	13.84	16.64	61
63	12.81	11.81	12.05	12.72	15.30	63
65	11.79	10.88	10.97	11.63	14.00	65
67	10.75	9.96	9.96	10.61	12.76	67
70	9.18	8.60	8.54	9.22	10.99	70
73	7.72	7.33	7.26	7.96	9.41	73
75	7.01	6.54	6.48	7.12	8.46	75
77	6.40	5.83	5.76	6.23	7.58	77
80	5.51	4.75	4.78	4.94	6.50	80
83	4.65	3.80	....	3.82	5.57	83
85	4.12	3.37	....	3.12	4.84	85
87	3.71	3.01	....	2.53	4.03	87
90	3.28	2.41	....	1.95	2.83	90

* Extracted, with slight omissions, from Popular Tables, etc., by C. M. Willich, edited by Montague Marriott: London, 1857, p. 76.

TABLE II.—Showing the Expectation of Life, or the Period an Individual of a given age may expect to live, according to the following Tables of Mortality, deduced from Observations made on the Continent of Europe.*

Completed Age.	SWEDEN.			FRANCE.		HOLLAND.	BRESLAU.	BRANDENBURG.	Completed Age.
	Males.	Females.	General Population.	General Population.	State Annuitants.	State Annuitants.			
0	33.19	35.70	34.42	28.76	34.89	34.47	27.45	30.68	0
1	41.96	44.00	42.96	36.35	45.67	41.77	33.43	37.60	1
5	45.62	48.00	46.80	43.40	48.35	44.45	41.20	42.94	5
10	43.95	46.26	45.07	40.80	46.92	42.71	40 40	42.14	10
13	42.00	44.26	43.11	38.74	45.08	40.90	38.68	40.05	13
15	40.56	42.77	41.64	37.40	43 66	39.55	37.40	38.64	15
17	39.10	41.30	40.18	36.11	42.25	38.19	36.11	37.22	17
20	36 96	39.15	38.03	34.26	40.29	36.31	34.15	35.07	20
23	34.94	37.01	35.96	32.48	38.43	34.41	32.22	33.10	23
25	33.64	35 58	34.59	31.33	37.21	33.28	30.88	31.76	25
27	32.33	34.18	33.23	30.20	36.02	32.36	29.64	30.55	27
30	30.33	32.17	31.23	28.52	34.18	30.93	27.81	28.70	30
33	28.40	30.27	29.30	26 84	32.26	29.49	26.05	26.83	33
35	27.09	29.03	28.03	25.72	30.95	28.36	24 92	25 56	35
37	25.77	27.69	26.70	24.59	29.62	27.22	23.83	24.41	37
40	23.75	25.63	24.66	22.89	27.54	25.50	22.19	22.65	40
43	21.89	23.78	22.80	21.18	25.42	23 62	20.57	20 86	43
45	20.71	22.57	21.61	20.05	24.02	22.34	19.56	19.65	45
47	19.69	21.28	20.37	18.91	22.61	21.13	18.54	18.43	47
49	18.31	19.23	19.08	17.79	21.21	19.99	17.53	17.18	49
50	17.72	19.26	18.46	17.23	20.51	19.41	17.07	16.55	50
51	17.18	18.62	17.87	16.67	19.83	18.87	16.61	15 96	51
53	16.09	17.39	16.70	15.58	18.45	17.82	15.71	14.78	53
55	14.99	16.16	15.54	14.51	17.15	16.73	14.77	13.68	55
57	13.87	14.90	14.36	13.46	15.92	15.66	13.78	12.68	57
59	12.79	13.67	13.20	12.45	14.70	14.62	12.80	11.73	59
60	12.25	13.08	12.63	11 95	14.15	14.17	12.30	11.28	60
61	11.72	12.54	12.10	11.47	13.59	13.58	11.81	10.84	61
63	10.74	11.51	11.09	10.53	12.52	12.54	10.83	9.98	63
65	9.78	10.49	10.10	9.63	11.43	11.56	9.86	9.15	65
67	8.84	9.47	9.12	8.77	10.37	10.59	8.89	8.38	67
70	7.60	7.92	7.72	7.58	8.79	9.15	7.45	7.39	70
73	6.53	6.63	6.53	6.51	7.29	7.74	6.25	6.52	73
75	5.89	6.03	5.91	5.86	6 44	6.82	5.51	6.17	75
77	5.26	5.43	5.29	5.29	5.71	6.02	4.84	5.76	77
80	4.27	4.46	4.28	4.60	4.73	5.06	4.08	5.06	80
83	3.45	3.59	3.57	4.19	3.86	4.09	3.19	4.55	83
85	3.16	3.40	3.23	4.16	3.33	3.38	3.37	4.19	85
87	2.88	3.23	2.92	4.28	2.72	2.84	1.62	3.61	87
90	2.02	2.55	2.05	3.86	1.77	2.47	0.50	2.50	90

* Extracted, with slight omissions, from Popular Tables, etc., by C. M. Willich. Edited by Montague Marriott: London, 1857, p. 76.

TABLE III.—Rates of Mortality and Expectation of Life in the United States of America.*

Age.	Number Living.	Number Dying.	Expectation of Life.
10	100,000	749	48.72
13	97,762	740	46.82
15	96,285	735	45.50
17	94,818	729	44.19
20	92,637	723	42.20
23	90,471	720	40.17
25	89,032	718	38.81
27	87,596	718	37.43
30	85,441	720	35.33
33	82,277	726	33.21
35	81,822	732	31.78
37	80,353	742	30.35
40	78,106	765	28.18
43	75,782	797	25.99
45	74,173	828	24.54
47	72,497	870	33.08
49	70,731	927	21.63
50	69,804	962	20.91
51	68,842	1,001	20.20
53	66,797	1,091	18.79
55	64,563	1,199	17.40
57	62,104	1,325	16.05
59	59,385	1,468	14.74
60	57,917	1,546	14.09
61	56,371	1,628	13.47
63	53,030	1,800	12.26
65	49,341	1,980	11.10
67	45,291	2,158	10.00
70	38,569	2,391	8.48
73	31,243	2,505	7.10
75	26,237	2,476	6.28
77	21,330	2,369	5.48
80	14,474	2,091	4.38
83	8,603	1,648	3.39
85	5,485	1,292	2.77
87	3,079	933	2.19
90	847	385	1.42

* Reduced from Medical Examinations for Life Insurance by J. A. Allen, M.D., New York: 1872, p. 157.

These tables offer much food for reflection and speculation, which this is not the place to enter upon; but the reader cannot fail to be struck with the third table, according to which the expectation of our American cousins appears to be higher than our own. Is the race of life really less exhausting in the United States than on this side of the Atlantic?

For a long time it appeared as if an antagonism existed between the medical profession and insurance companies, which was due to the fact that the companies expected the medical attendants of the insurees to communicate to them the medical history of their patients without the customary honorarium. This could only be regarded as unreasonable, as, for their own greater security, the companies asked for information from medical men, which was to enable them to judge of the eligibility of a particular life. All difficulties of this kind are now removed, and as the information is given with the consent of the candidate for insurance, no breach of confidence can be imputed. It is now universally admitted by all parties interested, that the medical element constitutes an important item in the consideration of a proposal for life insurance; and that although the regular medical adviser of the company is able, by inquiry and observation, to elicit many points that determine the issue, much may elude his vigilance, owing to the necessary limits of time and space, and also from the reticence, wilful or accidental, which many people exercise on matters of health. For this reason it is deemed essential by some of the best offices to obtain particulars as to previous illnesses, hereditary data, and habits, from the gentleman who has been regarded as the applicant's professional adviser.

The object of the following chapters is to point out those features in the constitution, sanitary condition, family predisposition, and mode of life, of applicants for insurance, to which medical men have to pay special attention. To those who doubt the value of information to the managers of insurance companies obtainable by careful medical examinations, we would address the remarks made by Sir Robert Christison in 1853.* By comparing the mortality among the insured in the Standard Life Office with the mortality from similar causes occurring in the population at large, the author arrives at the conclusion that an assurance company may expect to be relieved of a considerable number of casualties, which must affect its operations under a looser procedure, and he continues:—"If a collection of select lives be no better than the average, a collection of inferior lives cannot be worse; consequently a believer in the inutility of choosing good lives must be prepared to deal with the assurance of none but picked bad ones; but a scrutiny of the last quinquennium of the Standard Company supplies positive evidence of the positive advantage of a reasonable amount of care in accepting proposals." †

* An Investigation of the Deaths in the Standard Assurance Company, by Robert Christison, M. D., in Edinburgh Monthly Journal, August 1853.

† The following remarks by a distinguished actuary on this

The common opinion of all who have had much similar experience confirms the justice of the dis-

question deserve the attention of every friend and promoter of life insurance:—Mr. Griffith Davies (on Annuities) says: "That a very considerable advantage accrues to an insurance office by the rejection of bad lives is too evident to be denied; for without this caution there is reason to suspect that assured lives would be worse than the average, as their acceptance could not fail to induce persons of weak constitution to have recourse to life assurance for the benefit of their survivors; while those of robust health might think it more to their advantage to improve their own savings for the advantage of their families. But whether the selection from the class of persons composing the majority of those who have recourse to life assurances renders them better than the average is not so evident; as it will appear by the Table herein deduced from the experience of the Equitable, that the mortality among the members of that institution approximated exceedingly near to that which obtained during the same period among the inhabitants of the town of Carlisle, shown by Mr. Milne's table, which there is reason to believe, with its author, affords a pretty fair index of the contemporaneous mortality among the community at large throughout England and Wales. But even granting the mortality among the members of the Equitable to have been considerably less than the average among the community at large, the present competition, and the possibility of fraud attending the practice of employing agents and medical examiners in distant parts of the Empire, not only increases the expense, but renders it doubtful whether, even with the advantage of a greater number of country lives, the persons assured by other institutions are likely to average an equal longevity." This opinion was expressed more than forty years ago. The change which steam has since wrought in the social relations would probably have caused the author to modify it somewhat had he survived to witness the revolution that has taken place in human intercourse through railways and steamboats, the introduction of the penny postage, and the spread of education.

tinguished professor's statement; but for the benefit of those who do not enjoy the opportunities of personal observation, we may quote an illustration given by the late Dr. Brinton.* He examined a number of insurances effected without medical examination. From three or four pages of these cases he collected no less than forty instances of death by pulmonary consumption, at periods which averaged eighteen weeks from the date of effecting the policy, but often did not exceed three, four, or five weeks. The average loss to the Society on these forty policies was exactly forty times the premiums paid.

* On the Medical Selection of Lives for Assurance, by W. Brinton, M. D., 1856. Second edition.

CHAPTER II.

THE NORMAL MAN.

WERE insurances effected upon every member of the community indiscriminately, and did every company take its due proportionate share, the risk and the result could be calculated with absolute certainty, as the duration or prospect of life of each member of the community can be accurately determined. But the nature of our social relations makes it necessary that the lives taken by insurance companies should be selected lives, and that they should approach as nearly as possible to a standard of perfect health. * Although in all well-regulated States the statistics referable to the entire population are reliable even to minute details, the individual is subject to accidents which cannot be foreseen or calculated, and therefore, as only a limited number of people appreciate the value

*For details connected with, and in illustration of, this train of thought, the reader will do well to refer to an admirable treatise by Dr. J. G. Fleming, of Glasgow, entitled Medical Statistics of Life Assurance. Glasgow, 1862. The work is unfortunately out of print, and we have had much difficulty in obtaining a copy for reference. In a careful analysis of the deaths and causes of death occurring in thirty-six years in the Scottish Amicable Society, Dr. Fleming places before his readers numerous interesting and important conclusions, some of which we shall take the opportunity of reproducing in our pages.

of life insurance, and there are always many who would be willing to benefit themselves to the detriment of the insurance company, it is necessary that the latter should be on its guard against involuntary deception or actual fraud. A company that took no precautions as to selecting average lives would, as has been repeatedly the case, soon find its assets incapable of covering its liabilities. And one of the first conditions of successful life insurance business is, that there should be no doubt as to its being at any time able to fulfil its engagements towards those who have invested their money in premiums with a view to securing for themselves or their successors a stipulated benefit.

It is equally to the interest of the insurer and the policyholder that every guarantee should be obtained that the latter offers all the conditions of good health, which means that he possesses no hereditary taint, and that his organs and functions are in a condition to enable him to bear the wear and tear of life without unnecessary detriment. He should approach as nearly as possible the ideal or typical man, the limit of whose age may reasonably be assumed to lie somewhere between 70 and 80.* Practically it is impossible to insure perfect health in a large number of insurers, though Dr. Fleming and others show that in the aggregate their rate of

* This agrees with the scriptural threescore years and ten, but it is to be observed that in Genesis (vi. 3,) the days of man are promised to be one hundred and twenty years. Flourens and Buffon are both of opinion that the natural term of existence is one hundred years.

mortality is lower than that occurring among the general population. The influences that we are all subject to, owing to the hereditary impress we receive before birth, the neglect of sanitary laws, the friction we undergo in our passage through life, the labour and anxiety associated with existence, impair in the individual, to a great extent, the standard of perfect health, which theoretically may be attained. For this deviation the tables of insurance premiums are calculated to make due allowance; for if there were not a proper margin for the accidents of life, no insurance business could be safely conducted, and it is, even with that condition, necessary to have large averages, in order to secure permanence and stability.

Before proceeding to the consideration of those elements which impair the prospect of life and diminish the working capabilities of our organism, it may be well to devote some space to the examination of the conditions which constitute perfect health, and of the means at our disposal to determine their existence. It is the departure from these conditions that constitutes the real difficulty of the medical referees of life insurance associations, who are bound to reverse the legal theory that every man is innocent until he be proved guilty, and to assume that every candidate for insurance is more or less unsound until his physical health is conclusively established.

We cannot regard the individual as self-contained. From the earliest history of man the influences imparted by progenitors to their descendants have been recognized; and though such influences may be neutralised or modified by training and education, they will ever imperatively demand a large share in the estimate of individual quality and character. The Mosaic account of the origin and development of the Jewish race has a red line of genealogical doctrine running through it, which presents features of the greatest interest to the student of mankind, while the "Fortes creantur fortibus et bonis" of Horace is only one of the many instances of a recognition of the same principle by profane writers of antiquity, which has received larger and more scientific treatment by philosophic inquirers of recent times.

For the purpose of life insurance it is necessary to determine the existence and the character of hereditary influence from three aspects. The evidence obtainable may be derived from preceding generati ns, from collaterals, and from descendants. It has been too much the custom to pay regard only to the vital power of progenitors; but important as this point is, we shall find, when discussing special morbid taints, that the health of collaterals offers very valuable indications as to the health of an insuree, which are not afforded or not accessible when the former alone is examined. The condition of descendants, in the nature of things, does not so frequently assist in determining the health of their predecessors, because, though theoretically of similar import, the age of insurers generally militates against this element becoming an item in the calculation of their vital power. Apart from the actual health of the progenitors, physiological conditions come into play, that frequently determine the viability of their offspring, some of which at least are readily ascertainable. To these belong the relative ages of the parents at the time of the insuree's birth. Great disparity of age is justly regarded as exercising a prejudical influence, even though other points are favourable. Blood relationship, again, which in this country is not a bar to marriage in degrees that physiologically are objectionable, leads to the production of a sickly offspring, which may not at the time of insurance have exhibited any failure of power, but which nevertheless would be less capable of resisting morbid influences, to which they must sooner or later be subjected. It is this power of resisting disease, the *vis insita*, to which in all cases the medical referee's attention requires to be specially directed. The actual malady or morbid taint is comparatively easy of detection, but the gauge that is to test the insuree lies in the means of estimating his ability to undergo the heat and burden of active life, and to ward off or bear with impunity the noxious influences which he cannot altogether escape.

In the increasing intercourse among the nations of the world, and the intermarriage between different races, considerations may be expected to arise, which, with the spread of life insurance to the dependencies of Great Britain, will merit future discussion. The deterioration of race in various parts of the globe has already attracted attention, and it is an acknowledged fact that the burgher population of

Ceylon, descended from the earlier Dutch settlers, no longer presents the sturdy characteristics of their forefathers. As yet, fortunately, we possess no analogous declension in any British community; but the locality of birth, even where the parents are healthy, already deserves the attention of the medical referee in the examination of English lives. Whether, in the course of time,* a change in the habits, and the adoption of hygienic measures not yet appreciated, may modify the effect of climate, remains to be seen; but for the present it is an undoubted fact that the healthy children of healthy English parents born in tropical regions, after a few years pine away, and unless sent to temperate zones,

* That such an anticipation is reasonable, is borne out by facts already at our disposal; thus it is found that although, according to the sanitary report of the Bengal Presidency for 1871, the death of European children in the plain of India, amounts to 91·4 per 1000, the mortality at a school in Rajpootana, in existence since 1854, on Mount Aboo, has only been 8 per 1000. The site of the school is 4500 feet above the level of the sea, and enjoys a mean temperature of 69° F. In order to show the contrast between the ordinary mortality of English children brought up in England and India respectively, we annex the following tabular statement of their death-rates, compiled by Dr. Fayrer (*Brit. Med. Journ.*, May 3, 1873).

	England.	India.	
Under five years .	67·58 ...	148·10	per 1000.
Five to ten years .	8·80 ...	17·73	"
Ten to fifteen years .	4·98 ...	11·51	"

We experience some doubt as to these numbers being correct, as the mortality for the children in England is manifestly too low; but Dr. Fayrer's authority stands too high to doubt the general results to which the table points.

lose the vigour which is their inheritance. The longer their return is delayed, the greater will be, cæteris paribus, the impairment of vital power, which, apart from actual disease, will tend unfavourably to modify this susceptibility to disease, and to diminish their prospects of longevity.

As regards temporary residence in various countries, it is questionable whether, in the present state of social intercourse, and with the improved methods of communication and sanitary appliances of all kinds, it can be considered as affecting life insurance prejudicially. Messrs. Bailey and Day* show, in opposition to Dr. Guy, that the members of the peerage enjoy a high average duration of life, and remark that the male lives of that class enter the army and navy in large numbers, travel extensively, and are more exposed to what assurance offices consider extra risks, than the middle classes. They infer that differences of climate have less effect on human mortality than differences of occupation and position in life, and that, as the offices do not attach much importance to the latter, they might relax somewhat in their estimate of the former. We willingly adopt the corollary without the reason assigned, for we hold that offices ought to be more particular than they are in considering the influence of occupation on the expectation of life.

Physically, as well as morally, the child is undoubtedly "the father of the man." Everything, therefore, that aids in the normal growth of the

* On the Rate of Mortality amongst the Families of the Peerage.—*Assurance Magazine*, July 1861.

infant, materially affects its future well-being. Hot-house plants, and plants overstimulated by rich manure, are the exact prototypes of children reared in a manner calculated to anticipate the normal periods of development. The laws of nature are not difficult to read that bear upon this matter; and were it possible to go into the question of early training of our applicants for insurance, we should doubtless be able to fix, with greater certainty than we now possess, their future chances of life. I allude more particularly to the feeding of infants,* to the prejudicial influence of hand-feeding, adopted for various reasons to which it is unnecessary to allude here, in lieu of the only physiologically correct food for infants, the maternal milk. During the later periods of childhood, the employment of artificial stimuli of all kinds, physical, emotional, and intellectual, largely impairs brain-growth, muscle-growth, blood-growth, either by a development of one part of the organism at the expense of another, or by directly stunting the entire process of nutrition.

We need scarcely dwell longer on the aspects of childhood in reference to life insurance at present. Although some offices present an attractive feature with reference to early insurance, by which the premiums are returnable if death occurs before the age of 21, this very arrangement renders as close an

* Those who wish to study the laws governing the nutrition and development of the child, are particularly referred for valuable information to Dr. Edward Smith's elaborate work on Health and Disease, as influenced by the Daily, Seasonal, and other Cyclical Changes in the Human System: London, 1861.

investigation into the antecedents of the child less necessary than it becomes during the periods of life after growth is completed, and when applications for insurance are most largely made. But when manhood is established, the question of the extent to which, within the limits of health, variations of structure and function may exist, become of paramount importance; and it is here that we particularly look for a standard of comparison by which to determine the departure from the typical man, without recognizing a positively morbid condition.

The remarks that follow are chiefly the result of observations made upon members of that somewhat complex race to which the modern Briton* belongs; and as he is not regarded as inferior to any of his contemporaries, whatever is true in him may be applicable to mankind at large.

The period of complete manhood is fixed by law at 21; but physiologically this is certainly not universally correct, for although development may be regarded as accomplished in every respect at this age in the healthy English female, and vertical growth may have terminated even in the male, a man's vital power cannot be regarded as having

*This term is used advisedly, because there are observed differences between the three chief divisions of the inhabitants of Great Britain; and if the term Englishman were employed here, it might lay the writer open to the imputation of wishing to ignore features indicating a physical superiority of the Scotchman or the Irishman. For the purpose in view, such a distinction would be unnecessary.

attained its maximum development until about the age of 30.* For some years after the youth has ceased to grow, in the ordinary sense of the word, the dimensions of his chest, the great index of vital power, continue to expand, and numerous are the instances derived from military experience, showing that recruits at the age of 20 are unable to undergo the fatigue of active service, that is borne with impunity by men of a more mature age.† They are literally not as yet well knit together. Several important bones are not perfectly consolidated, and it may be specially mentioned that the sternum, which has to bear so great a strain in laboured respiration, and is specially taxed by the weight of the soldier's knapsack, is not converted into a single plate of bone until after the thirtieth year. It is not until the sixth quinquennial period of life that our leading anatomical authorities find that the following events, connected with the consolidation of the skeleton, take place:—1. Completion of the vertebral column; 2. Completion of the sacrum; 3. Coalescence of the third with the second piece of

*Quetelet (Sur l'Homme et le Développement du ses Facultés, Paris, 1835) shows that the growth of man cannot be regarded as universally complete at the age of 25; see his Tables of Measurement taken on inhabitants of Bruxelles, vol. ii. p. 13. Quetelet also gives tables showing the completion of female growth at 20, and the completion of male growth at 30.

†For detailed information upon this point, the reader is especially referred to Professor Aitken's work, on the Growth of the Recruit: 1862.

the sternum; 4. Completion of the ribs; and 5. Coalescence of the haunch-bones with their crests.

The average height of an Englishman brought up under favourable circumstances is 5 feet $9\frac{3}{5}$ inches, which is notably above that of the average Belgian, Frenchman, or Italian. The height of the average English female appears to be about 5 feet 2 inches.* It would be difficult to fix the limits at which height and health are incompatible. The downward range is certainly larger than the upward range, which appears due to the fact that the vital organs, the heart, and the chylopoietic viscera, do not keep pace in development with the muscular and osseous systems of persons exceeding the normal elevation. We more frequently meet with people of diminutive stature, with a perfectly equable development of external and internal organs, who, for purposes of life insurance, would offer every reasonable guarantee for their viability, than with men and women materially exceeding the average stature, in whom some invalidating element in the organs of sanguification, circulation, and innervation, may not be traced. Cæteris paribus, the small person is more easily nourished, and if, at the same time, the respiratory function is well carried on, which we shall shortly see is one of the most assured signs of vigour, he is on the whole better adapted for the warfare of life than his overgrown neighbour, to whom, possibly, he may look up with envy.

We will next examine the bearing of the weight

* Cowell's Factory Reports, quoted by Quetelet, vol. ii. p. 18.

of the individual upon health. Here we find, normally, a progressive increase from birth to the decline of life, which must not be regarded as identical with development, as we have seen that the full growth of the body reaches its acme in the third decennium of life. The increase of weight that takes place at a later period is due to the accumulation of fat under the skin and in the cavities of the body, and, as is well known, very commonly assumes morbid proportions, which often affect the life insurance value of the individual. From birth * the male sex exceeds the female, both in size as well as weight, and this prevails throughout life excepting, according to Quetelet, † at the age of 12, when the weight of both is the same ; but it appears, according to the same authority, that the female attains her maximum of weight at a later period of life than the male.

According to Liharzik, ‡ the normal growth of the human body is completed at the end of the 25th year. He estimates the mean height of a "growing lad" at 18 years at 163 centimètres, or 64·17 inches, and that of a man who has completed his normal growth at 68·9 inches.

The average weight of a young Englishman of 21 is 151 lbs., but the table in ordinary use to determine the normal height and weight of applicants for insurance is given for the age of 30, at

* Quetelet, vol. ii. pp. 8 and 35, *et seqq.* † Vol. ii. p. 47.

‡ Law of Increase, by F. P. Liharzik, M. D.: 1862. See also Aitken's Growth of the Recruit, and Dawson in *Statistical Journal*, March 1862.

which there is already an increase upon the former estimate; it will also be seen that the average increase per inch of stature above 5 feet is $5\frac{1}{6}$ lbs., although the range of variation at the different heights is greater than might have been supposed *a priori.*

Model Heights and Weights.

Age 30.

The Height being				The Weight should be			
5	feet	1	inch . . .	8	stone	4	lbs.
5	,,	2	,, . . .	9	,,	0	,,
5	,,	3	,, . . .	9	,,	7	,,
2	,,	4	,, . . .	9	,,	13	,,
5	,,	5	,, . . .	10	,,	2	,,
5	,,	6	,, . . .	10	,,	5	,,
5	,,	7	,, . . .	10	,,	8	,,
5	,,	8	,, . . .	11	,,	1	,,
5	,,	9	,, . . .	11	,,	8	,,
5	,,	10	,, . . .	12	,,	1	,,
5	,,	11	,, . . .	12	,,	6	,,
6	,,	0	,, . . .	12	,,	10	,,

Although the standard supplied by this table may be regarded as a valuable indication of the individual's health, it must not be relied upon alone as a test of his suitability for insurance. Considerable variations occur within limits that do not impair the prospect of longevity; but where they are marked, greater care is requisite to determine the value of other points that bear upon the viability of the person under examination. Such variations depend upon race, employment, age, habits of life, sex, and temperament, which, from the absence of sufficient data, it would be impossible to formularise, but which, nevertheless, are roughly taken into consideration in estimating the value of a life. We all know that a Scotchman does not yield in bodily or mental vigour to the Englishman, yet experience teaches us that the average weight of the former is less than that of the latter.* Dr. James Forbes, when Professor of Natural Philosophy in Edinburgh, examined 800 students with reference to their physical development, distinguishing the natives of England, Scotland, and Ireland. He found the law established that development in every respect increases between 14 up to 26 years of age, but that the increase became slower as the age advanced. Our Scotch friends will be pleased to hear that, tested by Regnier's dynamometer, Scotchmen were superior to Englishmen in tractile power. This being measured by pounds gives for

Englishmen at the age of	20 to 55,	366 to 384 lbs.
Scotchmen	,,	,,	374 ,, 404 ,,
Irishmen	,,	,,	397 ,, 413 ,,

Sedentary occupations, with an ample food-supply, tend to increase the weight, while it is reduced by employment involving continued open-air exercise and a tax upon the muscular system. An undue diminution of weight would be regarded with more suspicion early in life, as indicating impaired nutrition, and taken with any symptom, not by itself adequate to raise a doubt, that tended in the same direction, might justify rejection. On the other

* Aitken's Growth of the Recruit, pp. 44 and 71.

hand, an abnormal elevation of weight when manhood is established, though compatible with health if the occupation and mode of life be healthy, may imply a tendency to fatty degeneration, or to apoplectic affections where the concurrent circumstances are not equally favourable. In all these questions a certain latitude is unavoidable, and what is technically called circumstantial evidence must guide the inquirer in arriving at a conclusion. Dr. Purdon, in a recent pamphlet on life insurance, following Dr. Brinton,* allows a variation of 20 per cent as compatible with health. This may be exceptionally true, but, practically, it is found where early deaths occur from constitutional disease that a smaller variation than this implies ought, at the time of insurance, to have attracted attention and commanded an increased rate, although no other indication of a hereditary or constitutional taint existed. Our own experience leads us more and more to regard the table as a valuable aid in determining the value of an applicant's life, and we regard with suspicion any material departure from the law it appears to involve.

Any sudden change of weight demands still more careful consideration than a habitual departure from the normal standard. It may, as in an obese person, be the result of an illness that restores a healthy state of things, but it is more frequently the forerunner of disease; when it takes the form of reduction, we look for some morbid taint that

* On the Medical Selection of Lives for Assurance, 2d edition, 1856.

induces wasting, as consumption; where it runs in the opposite direction, the prospect of life may be affected by alcoholism, by degeneration of the vessels, leading to cardiac, renal, or cerebral mischief, or by some analogous impairment of the nutritive powers.

A very interesting table, showing the relation between height and weight, was compiled about twenty years ago by Mr. Hutchinson,* based on an examination of 3000 males. It is buried in a valuable article on respiration, published in a professional volume of Transactions, and is therefore not easily accessible. Moreover, as it applies to lives varying in age from 15 to 40, it does not serve the purposes of life insurance so well as one which refers to the age of thirty, when, for all practical considerations, development may be said to have attained its acme. Still, as Mr. Hutchinson's researches have afforded the main basis for establishing this particular feature in connection with an estimate of health, and as his claims as an original worker are frequently ignored, we reproduce his table here. We premise that the classes whence he took his materials were sailors, firemen, metropolitan police, Thames police, paupers, artisans, labourers, Grenadier Guards, Horse Guards, printers, draymen, wrestlers, pugilists, Oxford and Cambridge rowers, London watermen, cricketers, pedestrians,

* On the Capacity of the Lungs and on the Respiratory Functions. — *Medico - Chirurgical Transactions*, vol. xxix. p. 137. 1846.

and gentlemen; a list sufficient to justify the belief that the results afford a fair average of the population.

Height.							No. of cases.	Gross weight in lbs.	Mean weight in lbs.
4 ft.	6	in. to	5	ft.	0	in.	26	2,399	92·26
5	0	,,	5		1		17	1,964	115·52
5	1	,,	5		2		36	4,476	124·33
5	2	,,	5		3		43	5,497	127·86
5	3	,,	5		4		88	12,145	138·01
5	4	,,	5		5		126	17,537	139·17
5	5	,,	5		6		214	31,016	144·93
5	6	,,	5		7		316	45,598	144·29
5	7	,,	5		8		379	57,822	152·59
5	8	,,	5		9		468	73,835	157·76
5	9	,,	5		10		368	61,238	166·40
5	10	,,	5		11		348	59,460	170·86
5	11	,,	6		0		245	43,475	177·45
6	6	,,	0		0		326	71,283	218·66
							3060	488,745	147·86

According to this table the average adult Englishman would weigh (say) 148 lbs.; but if we calculate the average from the weights given for the heights ranging from 5 feet 6 inches to 6 feet, both inclusive, we obtain the average of 161·5 lbs., which may be regarded as more closely approximate to the truth.

Of all the points bearing upon the present health and the future prospects of an individual, there is probably none that exercises a greater influence, and more deserves our attention, than his respiratory power as indicated by the development of his chest and its contents. Here again we are largely indebted to Mr. Hutchinson, whose table of heights and weights we have just quoted, but which forms only a very subordinate portion of the essay in which, with great research and minuteness, he investigates the relation between vital power and pulmonary capacity. It is fortunate that we possess more perfect means of gauging the power of the thoracic viscera, than are applicable to any other viscera of the body. We cannot only measure the external dimensions of the chest and determine the physiological movements of its walls, but we are able to watch the process carried on within, by the stethoscope and by percussion, by the spirometer, and by the sphygmometer, with results that amount to almost absolute certainty. In the ordinary inquiries necessary for life insurance, it is scarcely practicable to bring all these methods of research to bear upon every candidate for insurance. But there can be no doubt that, were we not afraid of frightening the customer, or were time no consideration, a more careful application of the various tests of pulmonary capacity would prevent many lives from being passed as normal, that now become claims at an earlier period than the medical examiner and his Board of Directors had reason to anticipate. Respiration and life may be regarded as synonymous, and we find that vital power may be measured by the manner in which the functions of respiration are carried on. Hence the stress that medical men, and even popular opinion, lays upon the value of a well-developed chest, which affords an indication of what Mr. Hutchinson was the first to term the vital capacity of the lungs. In ordinary quiet respiration the thorax is neither fully expanded, nor fully emptied of the contained air. To measure its entire capacity—*i.e.* to determine the whole amount of air which it is capable of taking in and discharging in one respiratory act*—it is necessary that a forced inspiration and a forced expiration should be made. Even after the latter act, a portion of "residual air" remains in the lungs, which is entirely independent of the will, and always present in the chest. Mr. Hutchinson terms the air of ordinary respiration "breathing air;" that of forced inspiration "complemental air;" and that of forced expiration "reserve air." The following table shows how widely previous observers had differed as to the quantity of air belonging to each of these divisions. They regarded

Residual air,	as ranging	from	40	to 260	cubic inches.
Reserve air	,, .	,,	77	170	,,
Breathing air	,,	,,	3	100	,,
Complemental air	,,	,,	119	200	,,
Vital capacity	,,	,,	108	300	,,

These discrepancies were due to Mr. Hutchinson's predecessors not having had regard to a variety of collateral circumstances which ought to be taken into account in estimating the process of respiration.

* It seems almost superfluous to insist upon the respiratory act consisting of inspiration and expiration. But as the frequency of respiration is required by most offices to be stated in their examination papers of candidates for assurance, it has occasionally happened to us to meet with replies of medical men, showing that even they treated inspiration and expiration as two distinct acts of respiration, which always gives a rate that in itself alone would suffice to justify rejection.

These are especially the power of the muscles concerned in respiration, the circumference of the chest, the height and weight of the individual, the pulse, the number of respirations, and the age.

We have already dwelt upon the questions of height and weight in assisting the determination of the normal conditions of the individual; we shall now see how the indications by these two elements receive further support in their relation to the vital capacity of the lungs. The greater advance we may make in inquiries of this nature, the more perfectly is the law of proportion that governs the typical man demonstrated; rendering it equally apparent how undue or imperfect development of any one organ or function throws the remaining organism out of gear, and constitutes a greater or less tendency to disease.

For a description of the methods, and especially of the spirometer, an instrument for measuring the air expelled during expiration, as well as for many details of great interest, we must refer the reader to the original paper by Mr. Hutchinson. It will suffice for the purpose of the present work to extract some of the chief practical results which he has attained.

The mean results of spirometrical measurements of the vital capacity of 1923 men, belonging to different classes of society, arranged according to height, together with their mean weights, are compiled in the following table, from which it will appear that there is a definite increase of vital

capacity closely proportionate to the increase in height:

Mean Vital Capacity of 1923 *Men belonging to different classes of society.*

Under 5 ft. . .	135 cubic in.	92·26 weight in lbs.
5 ft. 0 in. to 5 ft. 1 in.	175 „	115·52 „
5 „ 1 „ „ 5 „ 2 „	177 „	124·33 „
5 „ 2 „ „ 5 „ 3 „	189 „	127·86 „
5 „ 3 „ „ 5 „ 4 „	193 „	138·01 „
5 „ 4 „ „ 5 „ 5 „	201 „	139·17 „
5 „ 5 „ „ 5 „ 6 „	214 „	144·93 „
5 „ 6 „ „ 5 „ 7 „	229 „	144·29 „
5 „ 7 „ „ 5 „ 8 „	228 „	152·59 „
5 „ 8 „ „ 5 „ 9 „	237 „	157·76 „
5 „ 9 „ „ 5 „ 10 „	246 „	166·40 „
5 „ 10 „ „ 5 „ 11 „	247 „	170·86 „
5 „ 11 „ „ 5 „ 12 „	259 „	117·45 „
Over six feet	276 „	218·66 „

The mean for all heights being 217 cubic inches.*

When vital capacity is compared to weight, without reference to height, we fail to find the same progressive ratio of the respiratory power; thus the mean vital capacity of 147 men weighing 11 stone was 225 cubic inches; while that of 32 men of 14 stone only showed an increase of 8 cubic inches; so that, if there is, as we believe, a correlation between vitality or vital power and vital capacity, the man of lower weight has, cæteris paribus, the better prospect of longevity.

The vital capacity is found to increase from the age of 15 to 35, whereas from 35 to 65 it is de-

* The weights in the above table are the results obtained from a different and larger number of men than those examined for their vital capacity.

creased in the progression of 19, 11, and 13 cubic inches. It is remarkable, that although there is an exact relation between the circumference of the chest and weight, with which it increases in the exact arithmetic progression of 1 inch for every 10 lbs., Mr. Hutchinson was unable to find any such definite relation existing, as might be reasonably inferred, between the circumference of the chest and vital capacity. This result is so much opposed to the teachings of anatomy and vital dynamics, that although we cannot doubt the correctness of Mr. Hutchinson's observations, we think there must be some underlying fallacy dependent upon unobserved influences, or upon an insufficiency in the number of cases examined. Some of the points in his investigations have been confirmed in a remarkable manner by those of Dr. Balfour,* to whose researches we shall have an opportunity of alluding again, when we examine the bearing of spirometry upon chest-disease in connection with life insurance.

Very few remarks on the organs and functions of the body that we have not yet alluded to will bring to a close what we have to say in this chapter on the subject of the average man. There are no special tests by which we determine the healthy condition of the brain, or the abdominal viscera, as bearing upon life insurance. The absence of any morbid taint, which will form the subject of future chapters, must be taken as negative evidence of health, which is otherwise indicated by those evidences of

*Contributions to the Study of Spirometry, by J. G. Balfour, M.D., F.R.S.—*Medico-Chirurgical Transactions*, 1860.

normal development which we have recently discussed.

The decline of life * commences at periods which vary with the variations of hereditary and acquired vigour of the individual. Any exhausting influences that sap the powers of innervation or nutrition in youth and manhood will cause a premature senility, which, without actual disease, impairs the prospect of life of the individual. As a general rule, it is found that persons who have borne the battle of life well, and have passed the climacteric unscathed, are good subjects for insurance. The higher rates are, of course, calculated for the probable duration of life, but the casualties from unforseen disease are smaller than occur during the earlier decennia. Women have passed the dangers incidental to their sex, and men are no longer exposed to temptations and dangers which beset them in the heyday of youth and early manhood.

* It has often struck us of late years that it has become much more difficult to judge of the age both of ladies and gentlemen than we used to find it. This is doubtless in part due to the greater attention to sanitary laws; but our personal knowledge of the arcana of the toilet of many friends and patients compels us to believe that the dentist and the hairdresser have a great deal to do with the rarer appearance in the consulting-room of old people who "look their age." It might be a question whether the use of dyes, or, as they are euphemistically termed, restorers, washes, tinctures, balms, and what not, belongs to the venial deceptions practised in society, or whether insurance companies have a right to class them under the more opprobrious term of frauds. Perhaps we may consider ourselves living in a "Happy Land," where every "get up" is permissible which bears no allusion to political characters.

When we arrive at the consideration of the death of our typical man, it is melancholy to see how far in reality we are removed from the attainment of the end to which all sanitary science tends, in spite of the positive improvements which have demonstrably taken place since statistics have given us satisfactory data by which to judge of questions affecting the health of the population.

There is no natural termination of life but old age.

Yet we find by the Registrar-General's 14th and 15th annual reports, that of a total mortality for England of 395,396 from all causes in one year, only 25,996 were reported as having died of old age, or 6·5 per cent. The mortality in 1871 was 574,879, of which 28,038 were attributed to old age, or 5·4 per cent, a diminution that is more probably due to better diagnosis than to a change in the conditions of disease.*

It is to be feared that even this is much above the reality, for certificates of death are often given without adequate knowledge, and any physician of extensive experience will shrink from stating that anything like 6·5 per cent of deaths that have come under his personal knowledge could legitimately be set down to a simple wearing out of the vital powers, as implied by death from old age. We should be afraid to assert that we could attribute more than one of the many deaths that we have

* See Table of Causes of Death for the last Twenty Years, extracted from the Registrar-General's Reports for 1852-1871, at the end of this volume.

witnessed, during more than thirty years of professional life, to old age, strictly speaking; that is, where the termination of life could be attributed solely to the natural wearing out of the machinery, uncomplicated with active disease.

Hufeland, in his "Art of prolonging Life," asserts that no bachelors attain advanced age; and it is also stated that no idler, which means no man without a professed occupation, becomes very old. To both these rules the solitary instance in our memoranda formed a marked exception.

CHAPTER III.

THE DUTIES OF THE MEDICAL OFFICER.

THE regular employment of medical men to examine candidates for life insurance is a practice of comparatively recent date. The custom of the old offices, prior to about 1820, was for each life proposing, to sign a very distinct and binding declaration, to the effect that the individual had not had "cow or small pox, or any other disease tending to shorten life." No mention seems to have been made of family history. The proposer had to give a reference to "two persons of good repute, one, if possible, of the medical profession." Parties who did not appear before the directors, or who could not refer to a medical gentleman, were required to give a reference to three persons.*

Since that time the entire aspect of life insurance business has undergone a change; and while the companies have learned to appreciate the value of skilled medical advice, the members of the medical profession have acquired a direct pecuniary interest in promoting to their utmost the great social and

* See History and Constitution of the Equitable Society, by William Morgan, F.R.S.

economic principles which underlie insurance transactions. We have tried in vain to ascertain approximately the amount of honoraria paid in this way to the medical profession; but a little reflection will teach the reader that it must be very considerable, seeing that there is scarcely a medical man in the kingdom who is not more or less often applied to for his opinion as to the value of lives for insurance.

The duties which the medical officer of an insurance company undertakes to perform are of a very responsible character, as they involve both the happiness of the applicant and the welfare of the company. The rejection of a candidate not only interferes with his plans of making provision for his family, but implies the existence of a morbid taint or of actual disease, calculated to abridge his life, which he may not have suspected, and the revelation of which is likely to create serious alarm. If the examination is carefully conducted, and facts bearing upon the prospects of the life of the individual are overlooked or falsely estimated, the office will be mulcted by having to pay a claim before it ought to become due. A refusal to pay may be justified under circumstances of serious concealment, of actual fraud or conspiracy; but juries naturally tend to the side of the claimant's representatives, unless the evidence is of a very glaring character; and owing to the odium entailed, and to the consequent loss of business, companies shrink from appearing in court, unless they can bring overwhelming proof that they are the victims of deception, against which they had taken every possible precaution. The history of life assurance reveals many instances of gross frauds perpetrated upon life insurance companies; personation, forgery, and murder, have been employed, and frequently with success;* these are not generally matters for the professional consideration of the medical adviser, who has to guard chiefly against attempts at concealing facts that indicate depraved habits and a tainted constitution. In examining the statements made by the applicant and by his friends, he has to exercise discrimination and judgment, so as to note any discrepancies and to seize every indication of impaired vitality, which a single personal examination often fails to show. A case recently came under our notice in which an office successfully resisted the payment of a large claim on the ground of the concealment of facts, which certainly would have prevented the acceptance of the life had they been known when the policy was taken out. A gentleman died within a short time of effecting an insurance, at a distant continental watering-place. An accident suggested to the watchful and intelligent actuary that fraudulent representations had been made as to the deceased's previous health and habits. By following up the clue, and calling in the assistance of the detective department of the police, the deceased policyholder was shown to have been a victim of intemperance, through which he had, not long before effecting the insurance, become the inmate of the

* Ample illustrations are given in Mr. Francis' Annals, Anecdotes, and Legends of Life Assurance: London, 1853.

police cell, if not the lunatic asylum; and the collected evidence proved so conclusive, that instead of the company being called upon to pay a claim of £2000, it was mulcted only in the expenses of its inquiry. Tardieu* gives a curious illustration of the ingenuity brought to bear upon this species of fraud. A bankrupt, having assured his life in Paris in December 1864 for 100,000 francs, was reported soon after to have died in London of heart-disease, but it turned out that the policyholder had registered his own death in London, attended his own obsequies, and obtained a ship and cargo on the strength of the expected insurance. Murder and suicide have also, even in modern times, played a part in insurance business. Thus, for instance, we find in the same author a case of a Swede, Hoffstedt, who was insured by a man of the name of Swinson with the Caisse Paternelle in France, with the understanding that Swinson was to provide the former with brandy for the purpose of drinking himself to death. The brandy was not expeditious enough, so arsenic was administered. Fortunately this was discovered, and the policy cancelled.

We shall see that the question of temperance is one of great, and, unfortunately, very frequent difficulty. People entertain very different views as to where intemperance bégins, and, excepting where its effects have already left a permanent impress on the system, the indications are by no means such as to enable the medical examiner to trace its existence with certainty.

* Etude Médico-légale sur les Assurances sur la Vie. Paris, 1866, p. 109.

Although the necessity of a medical scrutiny into the value of all lives submitted for insurance is now an acknowledged fact, the manner in which the inquiry is conducted varies in different offices. The physician had little or nothing to do in the early days of insurance, which was then regarded in the light of any other contract between two individuals not necessitating the interference of skilled evidence. But as time wore on and the conditions of the contract became better understood, it was found that neither party was in a position to value the data upon which it was to be based, unless the state of health of the applicant and the various contingencies bearing upon his prospect of life were duly estimated. The physician now became an essential aid in the furtherance of life insurance business. It soon became apparent that although he might be fully competent to arrive at a satisfactory result by any method of examination that was most convenient to himself, it was necessary for future reference, as well as to enable the Board to form an opinion upon the various points at issue, that his reports should be made in a definite and uniform manner. Hence all offices now require the examination to be conducted according to a certain rule; and a fixed series of questions are issued, so that a record may be at hand which establishes both the bona fides of the policyholder and the manner in which the inquiry into his health was made.

The great difficulty in framing the queries has consisted in steering the middle course between pedantic minuteness on the one hand and too great breadth on the other. The former may prove vexatious to the applicant and irritating to the physician; but the latter may err by not suggesting subjects that a careless or much-occupied practitioner may slur over or forget. The medical man should remember that negative evidence is often as important as positive indications, and that while he has the opportunity of a personal interview with the applicant, the Board, who have to decide the rateable value of the life, do not possess this advantage. It often happens that the young practitioner, or one who knows little of the difficulties of framing a correct estimate of probabilities, resents the inquiries made by an office as an impertinence and as an imputation upon his mode of reporting; but any one who will bear in mind that, important as his functions may be, the decision must ultimately rest with the Board of Directors, and that they are responsible for the general business of the office, will also admit that they have a right to ask for such information as they may deem necessary to guide them. Many careless and slovenly reports have come to our notice, and this is the less to be justified now that the medical profession benefit pecuniarily to a very large extent by the system at present in force. It may be laid down as a general rule that the best men give the most satisfactory and detailed reports, as they fully appreciate the aid they afford towards the development of a social scheme of the highest value and importance.

The proposal for assurance, or the chief facts it contains, are submitted to the medical officer, and the statements subscribed to, on it, are useful data for comparison with the facts elicited by the examination; nor should the replies given by the proposer's friends be overlooked for the same reason. The manner in which they respond to the inquiry about the temperance of the applicant frequently affords a clue to further investigation, which he himself might withhold.

The age is an important element, not only as regards the amount of premium to be paid, but also in reference to the vis vitalis of the individual. It is proper that he should appear the age he assigns; but while it cannot be regarded as otherwise than generally favourable if he should look younger, it is decidedly the reverse if he looks much past his registered age, as this indicates precocious development in the young; and in those who have attained full manhood it is a sign of premature decay, depending, possibly, upon the anxiety and depression of business, upon exhausting diseases or excesses, or simply upon want of the normal vigour. In any of these cases the prospect of longevity would be reduced.

As the rates of insurance are based upon the calculated prospect of life at each age, the medical man need be under no apprehension in recommending persons of advanced age, who are in good average health, to insure. Our own experience accords with the conclusions arrived at by Mr. Neison, that the generally received opinion as to the insecurity of old lives * is fallacious, and that

* On the Medical Estimate of Life. for Life Assurance by Stephen Ward, M.D. London, 1857.

they are paying risks. They have passed through the dangers that beset early life, have learned how to take care of their health, and have probably attained that competency and contentment which are among the best guarantees for a prolonged existence.

The effects of intemperance, as proved by Mr. Neison, exhibit themselves chiefly at a comparatively early age, the maximum rate of mortality in intemperate lives occurring between 41 and 50, so that a person who at that age gives evidence of habitual temperance has escaped one of the most prevalent causes of degeneration of the tissued, and may boast of his age being

"As the lusty winter,
Frosty but kindly."

Tables of the calculated expectation of life ought to be in every medical practitioner's hands when he is called upon to give an opinion on the prospects of an individual. We shall subjoin one that is generally employed.

But there are easy methods for roughly determining the average expectation of life in England, such as that proposed by Mr. Willich.* He considers the expectation equal to two-thirds of the difference between the age of the individual and 80. Thus for a person aged 20, this difference would be 60, of which two-thirds, or 40, would give his probable duration of life.

* Quoted by Tardieu in Etude Médico-légale sur les Assurances sur la Vie: Paris, 1866; a translation, with notes of Dr. Taylor's Chapter on Life Assurance, in his Principles and Practice of Medical Jurisprudence, 1865. See also, Popular Tables, etc., by C. M. Willich, p. 176.

Mr. Walford* proposes a somewhat different procedure, which yields similar but not identical results. He directs us to use the fixed number 96, from which the ages ranging from 20 to 45 are to be deducted; the half of the remainder gives the expectance. According to his method, a person aged 20 would have an expectancy of 38; for 96 — 20 =76; this divided by 2, gives 38.

In order to approximate the result of the somewhat rough calculation previously given more closely to the Carlisle tables, Mr. Willich proposes the following expressions:—

From the age of 5 to 60—

$\frac{2}{3}$ of the difference between the age and $81\frac{1}{2}$ = expectation.

From the age of 60 to 74—

$\frac{1}{2}$ of the difference between the age and $88\frac{2}{3}$ = expectation.

From the age of 74 to 90—

$\frac{1}{4}$ the difference between the age of 103 = expectation.

None of these methods are quite accurate. When great precision is required, recourse must be had to Mr. Milne's mortality tables. The expectancy of life calculated by him, and known as the Carlisle tables, from the age of one to 80 are given on the following page:—

* Insurance Guide and Handbook, p. 163.

Average Duration of Life from 1 to 80 years of age, according to Carlisle Mortality.

Years old.	Expectancy. Years.	Years old.	Expectancy. Years.	Years old.	Expectancy. Years.
Birth	38¾	27	36½	54	18¼
1	44¾	28	35¾	55	17¾
2	47½	29	35	56	17
3	50	30	34½	57	16¼
4	50¾	31	33¾	58	15½
5	51¼	32	33	59	15
6	51¼	33	32½	60	14½
7	51	34	31¾	61	14
8	50¼	35	31	62	13½
9	49¾	36	30½	63	13
10	49	37	29¾	64	12½
11	48	38	29	65	11¾
12	47¼	39	28¼	66	11¼
13	46½	40	27¾	67	10¾
14	45¾	41	27	68	10¼
15	45	42	20½	69	9¾
16	44¼	43	25¾	70	9¼
17	43½	44	25¼	71	8¾
18	43	45	24½	72	8¼
19	42¼	46	24	73	7¾
20	41½	47	23¼	74	7¼
21	40¾	48	22½	75	7
22	40	49	22	76	6¾
23	39½	50	21¼	77	6½
23	38¾	51	20½	78	6¼
25	38	52	19¾	79	5¾
26	37¼	53	19	80	5½

After examining a life, the medical officer is expected to estimate, with all the data at his command, how far the individual's prospects appear to tally with the average; or what would, in the case of any deteriorating influences, be the fair allotment of advance upon the tabular rate. There must necessarily be much uncertainty in the conclusion arrived at; still it should not be regarded as mere guess-work, as increasing precision is the result of increased knowledge and experience. It would be well if every medical man, before advising the addition to the tabular rate on account of unfavourable family history or personal defect, were to ask himself what, under the circumstances, the probable duration of the applicant's life would be. By comparing his private estimate with the normal prospect of life at the applicant's age, and deducting the difference, he would at least show that his advice was based upon some intelligible principle. At present the suggestions offered by gentlemen of limited experience often show that they by no means appreciate the real question at issue, inasmuch as they state circumstances that materially affect the applicant's viability, and suggest additions to the tabular rate quite incommensurate with the manifestly increased risk to the office. Three or four years' addition is often recommended by medical men, where nothing less than ten or fifteen would cover the individual risk. What should be considered is, how much is a disease or defect in the family history of an individual likely to diminish his average longevity, as compared with a person without such a flaw in his antecedents. If the life is 30 and the answer is 10 years, the addition should be 15 years extra; *i.e.*, the expectation is 34½ at 30 and 24½ at 45, and the addition should be the difference between 30 and 45, or 15.

The occupation of the individual proposing to insure his life exercises an important bearing upon the estimate of his prospects. Some employments are more healthy than others; some offer more direct risk of accident or temptation; some promote the taint of disease discovered in an applicant; some tend to neutralise it. A person with a weak heart might be insurable if he belonged to such a station of life that he might be able to take all the requisite care; whereas if he were engaged in a laborious trade early death might be expected.

The residence is also to be considered, though, of course, no insurance company can bind its policy-holders to very narrow limits; and with the increased facility of communication, probably all restrictions will be modified if they cannot be entirely removed. As a general rule, town districts are less healthy than country districts; thus, in 1840, the annual mortality of every

1,000,000 in England was 27,073 in towns,
Do. do. 19,300 in country districts.

giving a difference against
town districts . . . 7,773

the population being in country districts 199, in town districts 5108 to the square mile.

The following table exhibits the great variations

that occur in the mortality of the population of England in different localities and occupations; the extremes of the averages show a variation of 19 years and 8 months between the healthiest and unhealthiest localities:—*

	The Gentry live.	Tradesmen live.	Laborers live.	General average.	
	Years.	Years.	Years.	Yrs.	Mon.
In Rutlandshire . .	52	41	38	43	8
Town of Truro . .	40	33	28	33	8
„ Derby . .	49	38	21	36	0
„ Manchester .	38	20	17	25	0
„ Bolton . .	34	23	18	25	0
„ Bethnal Green	45	26	16	29	0
„ Leeds . .	44	27	19	30	0
„ Liverpool .	35	22	15	24	0

When we go into more detail we find still greater variations among the various modes of life. Our sovereigns, with all the cares of their position and the risks it entails, show a better average than any sovereigns in the world, for the average duration of life of thirty-five successive English rulers is 52·03 years. It is, however, to be observed that their expectation on their accession to the throne was 33 years, so that the average ought to have been 63. The average duration of life of great statesmen is 56 years; but on the whole the professional classes present the most favourable aspect, considering the risks run and the harassing anxieties they submit to. Dr. Guy finds that the average life of the learned professions collectively is 76½ years, and he gives medical men the highest position, which is surprising to those who note the large number of deaths

* Walford, p. 75.

among students and young practitioners from diseases caught in the exercise of their profession.

Among the trades the mortality varies much—the most unfavourable occupations being those of the miner, the butcher, baker, and the inn and beer-shop keeper, as shown by the following statement of the Registrar-General. At the age of 45 to 55 the general mortality of England is 18 per 1000; but while of

1000	farmers . . .	12 died
,,	shoemakers . . .	15 ,,
,,	blacksmiths, carpenters, tailors, and labourers . .	17 ,,

we find that of

1000	miners* . . .	20 ,,
,,	bakers	21 ,,
,,	butchers . . .	23 ,,
,,	inn and beer-shop keepers .	28 ,,

For these trades, apart from any individual taint, an advanced rate may be fairly demanded. With the last category the mortality is so great, that many persons interested in life insurance would exclude them from its benefits altogether. Nothing, however, is more certain than the improvement of the sanitary condition and the prospect of life of the great bulk of the population; and, therefore, it is to be hoped that each of these trades will continue, as they have already done to a certain extent, to rectify

*Dr. Allen (Medical Examinations for Life Insurance, New York, 1872) puts the most dangerous trades in the following order:—1. Brakesmen on freight trains; 2. Burr sawyer; 3. Circular sawyer; 4. Powder-makers; 5. Seamen.

those sanitary irregularities which seem to be a part and parcel of their business. Mariners are, unfortunately, also "bad" lives; for while drowning is the cause of only 1 per cent of deaths in our male population, Mr. Harben* tells us that 35 per cent of deaths among seamen are attributable to accident. Among miners the proportion is 25; among engine attendants, 15; and among painters, plumbers, and glaziers it is 10 per cent. With regard to mariners, we would remark that this large mortality is essentially due to sea risks, and depends upon the dangers of wind and water, and not upon points directly affecting their expectation through disease. In speaking of the influence of railway travelling upon health, we shall place a table before the reader exhibiting the comparative liability to sickness which it appears to entail upon various members of the community. From this it is to be inferred that while railway officials lose a larger number of days by illness than any of the others, mariners are not only better off than this class, but enjoy a much greater immunity from sickness than the population at large. We do not know that this point has been duly considered by actuaries, for it would almost seem as if the two liabilities balanced one another.

The mortality in some of the trades has been materially diminished since public attention has been directed to the subject.

It is very encouraging to the medical profession, little public honour though it has received for its achievements, to find that owing to its energetic repre-

* Mortality Experience of the Prudential Assurance Company, by Henry Harben. 1871.

sentations the mortality in the army has been reduced considerably more than one-half within the last fifteen years. The mortality of the army—although it consisted of picked men, 30 to 40 per cent of the candidates for enlistment being rejected—was described by Deputy Inspector-General Marshall, more than twenty-five years ago, as presenting a higher rate of sickness and a greater mortality than that prevailing at the same period of life in the general population. It is creditable to the good sense of our authorities that, thanks to Professor Aitken, we are able to show national amendment in this respect, as exhibited in the following tabular view of deaths occurring annually between 1830 and 1836, and between 1859 to 1860, respectively, both at home and in our colonies:—

DEATHS AMONG THE TROOPS SERVING IN THE UNITED KINGDOM ANNUALLY PER 1000 MEN.

	1830 to 1836.	1859 to 1860.
Cavalry of the Line	15	6
Royal Artillery	15	7
Foot Guards	21	9
Infantry of the Line	17	8

The returns for the Colonies exhibited a similar reduction:—

	1837 to 1856.	1859 to 1861.
Gibraltar	22	9
Malta	18	14
Ionian Islands	27	9
Bermuda	35	11
Canada	20	10
Jamaica	128	27

Special rates are necessarily charged by all insurance companies for persons serving in or visiting tropical climates; and when they go to specially hazardous localities, like the West Coast of Equatorial Africa, insurances can only be effected under particular agreement. With regard to trades, it is the custom to add 10 to 20 per cent to the premium for innkeepers, for their trade alone ; a special rate is also universally adopted for all seafaring people, amounting generally to 25s. or 30s. on the sum assured. Other trades are not generally charged specially, but their influence on health and in developing any special taint, must be considered by the medical man. A laborious trade, for instance, would tend to foster the seeds of heart complaint, which in a person leading a very quiet life might cause no apprehension. A candidate showing a phthisical taint would be regarded more favourably if his occupation involved an open-air life rather than one of close confinement.

The question of Temperance is unfortunately one to which the special attention of medical officers has to be directed, both in the case of male and female candidates for insurance. The difficulty that we have to deal with consists in the very great latitude in the definition of intemperance. But for the purposes of life insurance the broad line may be laid down, that the habitual spirit-drinker, and especially one who is found to take strong drinks early in the day, ought to be declined altogether. The beer and wine drinker does not shorten his life frequently by excess, but there is scarcely a degenerative condition of the body that may not result from the abuse, or rather the habitual use, of ardent spirits.

It is doubtful whether teetotallers can be regarded

as very good lives, because they are frequently reformed drunkards; but when they have been advocates of the system before they had committed any excesses, or when they have taken the pledge before degenerative changes had occurred in the body, one cannot doubt that the teetotaller may be regarded as a good life. "The reformed drunkard," as Dr. Brinton * justly observes, "is not a good life; his repentance, as regards his physical constitution, often comes too late. Many months or even years of the most complete abstinence scarcely suffice to restore his probabilities of existence to a level with those of the temperate user of alcohol. Setting aside the not inconsiderable chances of his relapsing into old habits, his constitution often seems to have a peculiarly treacherous character; its apparently robust health consuming away with unusual rapidity under a moderately severe attack of any acute disease."

The medical man can scarcely expect to receive a denial of temperate habits from an applicant for insurance; but if, from the reports of friends, or from noting symptoms of dyspepsia, or from a history of "biliousness," a furred tongue, a quickened pulse, irregular flushing, tremulousness, and similar indications of alcoholic excesses, he suspects alcoholism, he must direct his questions to the exact frequency and quantity of the applicant's libations. Wherever the result of the inquiry is doubtful, the benefit of the doubt should be given to the company. The physician's gallantry must not mislead him when dyspeptic and anamalous nerve symptoms indicate alcoholism

* On the Medical Selection of Lives for Assurance, p. 18.

in the female ; unfortunately the vice of secret dram-drinking is met with in the best families, sometimes unknown to any but the victim ; at others it is recognised by members of the family, but is concealed * by them even from their medical attendant for very shame.

Excess in drinking is admitted by all physicians to be the frequent direct and indirect cause of fatal illnesses. Gluttony is less to be regarded as a cause of mischief, because the system more readily adapts itself to a certain excess of alimentary supplies ; and solid food not being so easily taken up and assimilated, a check takes place spontaneously to the introduction of more than a given quantity of solid food. The truly temperate man takes as much food and beverage as he requires for the due performance of all his functions, and not more of one or the other ; and the common experience of man, which is supported by scientific observation, is to the effect that our ordinary food goes farther and lasts longer if with it we consume a quantity of beer or wine, enough perhaps to exhilarate, but not sufficient to confuse or weaken the intellectual powers.

The questions generally put to the applicant for insurance embrace inquiries into his previous health, the health, or date of death, of his parents and brothers and sisters ; and, if it is a woman,

* This is a literal fact within the author's experience, who was called in to see a lady, in consultation, when she was moribund from alcoholic poisoning. The medical attendant, who had attended herself and other members of the family for years, had never before been called in to advise when she had suffered from slighter attacks of the same kind ; but on the occasion in question alarm was created, and the vicious propensities of the patient were revealed.

special inquiries are added with reference to utero-gestation and the uterine functions generally.

Life insurance is one of the indirect means by which vaccination is promoted, as it is always insisted upon where it is found to have been previously neglected.*

Female expectation is generally about three years in advance of males; but it does not appear that this advantage is perceived in life insurance, where the mortality among the female is larger than that of the male policyholders. The reader must form his own hypothesis as to the cause of this apparent contradiction; we fear he can scarcely arrive at a solution that is quite satisfactory. Unless a direct interest can be proved, as where the benefit of the wife's settlement is lost to the husband in case of her death, the husband can scarcely be permitted to insure his wife's life. Instances have come under our notice of early death having occurred after the rejection of an application by a husband to insure his wife; even when no foul play has occurred, it may be inferred that the husband was acquainted with some constitutional infirmity that was not generally apparent. The Married Woman's Property Act now enables a married woman to assure her own life under more convenient terms; and it may be confidently asserted that larger numbers of insur-

*It would be interesting if all the insurance offices would publish their experience with reference to smallpox. The author's experience leads him to fear that vaccination is often most inefficiently performed; for one office with which he is associated had no less than 18 claims during the recent epidemic, in consequence of deaths from smallpox in persons who had been vaccinated.

ances will be effected by females in consequence. The peculiar influences which render the lives of assured females worse than the unassured lives of males, seem worthy the attention of the medical man. Prior to 1772 they were charged more than males.

Parturition in the healthy female ought not to affect the prospect of life generally; and, excepting for primiparæ, is not generally regarded by insurance companies as justifying an advance upon the average premiums. The unfavourable statistics of parturition refer to periods and places where and when the sanitary laws were set at defiance or neglected, and when the value of pure air was ignored in lying-in rooms, as in the sick chamber generally; still the average is not now as favourable as it ought to be. The following table, compiled by Southwood Smith,* shows the fearful results, on the one hand, of the neglect of sanitary precautions, and, on the other, the comparative immunity from dangers of the parturient female under opposite conditions.—

Mortality of lying-in women in—

Hôtel Dieu, Paris	in 1786	1	in	15
Prussia	1817	1	in	112
British Lying-in Hospital, London	1750	1	in	42
Do. do.	1780	1	in	60
Do. do.	1789-1798	1	in	288
Lying-in Hospital, Dublin	1822	1	in	223
Town of Lewes	1820-1835	1	in	1205

It is to be regretted that Lewes can only be regarded as an exceptionally favourable specimen, because, according to Dr. Farr,† the general mortal-

* Philosophy of Health, vol. i. p. 139.

† Fifteenth Annual Report of the Registrar-General. Appendix, p. 69.

ity of parturient females was considerably greater at a much more recent period; he shows that in England one mother died for 192 children born alive, in the years 1851 and 1852. This average is improved when we take the longer period of twenty-five years from 1847 to 1871, during which, according to the Registrar-General's Report for 1871, published during the present year (1873), the number of deaths of mothers to 10,000 children born alive was 49, or 1 in 204 parturient women. Pregnancy has always been regarded as a woman's safeguard; but we should scarcely have been prepared for such complete immunity from fatal disease as indicated by the Registrar-General, who tells us that in 1871 only 35 pregnant women died.* The progressive improvement in the statistics of midwifery shown above is further borne out by the two following tables, which we borrow from Sir James Simpson's works.†

1. Average Number of Mothers dying in childbed in London, from 1660 to 1820.

1660 to 1680	.—1	death in every	44	delivered.
1680 to 1700	. 1	"	56	"
1700 to 1720	. 1	"	69	"
1720 to 1740	. 1	"	71	"
1740 to 1760	. 1	"	77	"
1760 to 1780	. 1	"	82	"
1780 to 1800	. 1	"	110	"
1800 to 1820	. 1	"	107	"

* Registrar-General's Report, 1871, p. 250.

† Obstetric Memoirs and Contributions, by James Y. Simpson, M.D. Edin. 1856, vol. ii. p. 543.

2. Proportion of Deaths in childbed in England and Wales, from 1839 to 1842.

Years.	No. of children born.	No. of mothers dying in childbed.	Proportion of maternal deaths in childbed.
1839	492,574	2915	1 in 169
1840	502,303	2989	1 in 168
1841	512,158	3007	1 in 170
1842	517,739	2687	1 in 182

In considering the influence of parturition upon the prospect of life of an individual, we may, excepting in the case of primiparæ, be guided by the account received of previous labours; and if they have been normal, we are not called upon to advise an advanced premium where the insurance is for the whole life.

When it is effected during pregnancy as for female lives generally, we have special regard to collateral circumstances, and inquire into the interest which a husband has, if he be taking out the policy. Strange revelations might be made under this head; but as they involve moral rather than medical considerations, they belong to the general history of life insurance,* and not to the topics to which it is desired to direct the reader's special attention.

An important distinction is to be drawn between primiparæ and multiparæ in regard to the danger of parturition. Dr. Allen † illustrates their

* Those curious in this peculiar development of moral obliquity will find ample food for reflection in The Annals, Anecdotes, and Legends of Life Assurance, by John Francis (London, 1853), which contains numerous illustrations of the frauds practiced upon life insurance companies.

† Medical Examinations for Life Insurance, by J. A. Allen, M.D.: New York, 1872, p. 175.

relative position by the following tabular statement, the details of which are collected from several sources :—

Authority.	No. of primiparæ.	No. of deaths.	*One death in every*	No. of multiparæ	No. of deaths.	*One death in every*
Hardy and Maclintock	2,125	35	**60**	4,510	30	**150**
Matthews and Duncan	3,722	50	**74**	12,671	103	**123**
Johnson and Sinclair	4,535	83	**54**	9,213	80	**115**
TOTALS	10,382	168	**62**	26,394	213	**124**

It follows from these statistics that, however much we may be disposed to regard parturition as a natural and healthy function, the human female is certainly exposed to a certain amount of danger, which, in those who have not borne children before, fully justifies insurance companies, irrespective of any other considerations, in charging a special rate, which, however, may be remitted when the process has been accomplished, or when the period of child-bearing has come to an end.

CHAPTER IV.

HEREDITARY INFLUENCES.

HAVING recently surveyed generally the medical aspects of life insurance, as indicated by the inquiries addressed to the candidate and his friends, we now proceed to a more detailed examination of the questions connected with the past history and the present health of the individual.

In the past history, the health and duration of life of his near relatives form most important items, involving as they do the influence which they exert by the hereditary transmission of good or bad qualities. The principle has been recognised from the earliest history of man by Scriptural authority and by profane writers, and is daily receiving fresh illustration and being made more precise in its practical application. The truth of Horace's

"Fortes creantur fortibus et bonis,"

no less than its converse, is daily verified by the records of life insurance. For this reason the inquiries addressed to a future policyholder as to his family history should never be lightly passed over. We constantly find that, even where the individual applicant presents an unimpeachable personal history, the hereditary taint manifests itself sooner or later in impaired vital power and in premature death.

We seek for evidence of inherited peculiarities in progenitors, in collaterals, in descendants, and in the person of the candidate for insurance. "As a general rule," we may say with Dr Guy,* "it will not be necessary to extend the inquiry beyond the father and mother, and the brothers and sisters, if the answers regarding them prove favourable; but if these near relations have died early, or if they appear to be subject to some hereditary malady, seriously affecting the duration of life, it may be necessary to include in the inquiry a larger circle of relationship."†

The question presents itself to us under two aspects, which we would consider as direct and as

*Principles of Forensic Medicine, by W. A. Guy, M.B., F.R.S., London, 1868, p. 139. See also, Aitken's Science and Practice of Medicine, vol. i. p. 392.

†Hippocrates evidently entertained a strong opinion as to the importance of hereditary influence. In his essay on the sacred disease, or what we term epilepsy, he says: "Its origin is hereditary, like that of other diseases. For if a phlegmatic person be born of a phlegmatic, and a bilious of a bilious, and phthisical of a phthisical, and one having spleen disease of another having disease of the spleen, what is to hinder it from happening, that when the father and mother are subject to this disease, certain of their offspring should be so affected also? As the semen comes from all parts of the body, healthy particles will come from healthy parts, and unhealthy from unhealthy parts." The last paragraph, though not expressed in the language of modern science, really contains the whole pith of the matter. (The whole works of Hippocrates, translated by Francis Adams, LL.D., Sydenham Society's Edition, vol. ii. p. 447.)

indirect hereditariness. The former implies the conveyance of a definite morbid taint from one generation to another; under the latter we understand the production of constitutional peculiarities not traceable to actual disease, but due to accidental circumstances affecting the embryonic condition of the individual, and influencing his future development. Many of the data are extremely difficult to obtain; and fortunately for mankind it is also true, that education and training may neutralise and divert the morbid impulse imparted to offspring; but the more the physician inquires into the private history of families, the more ground will he discover for his belief in the doctrine of hereditary influence. As yet, our knowledge on the subject is but very fragmentary, but it is one that largely concerns the schoolmaster, the political economist, and the philanthropist, as well as the physician; and it is to be desired that some Hercules in science may arise before long, not only able to gather up all the disjecta membra, but also to give shape and precision to many views that still possess no firmer basis than that of vague hypothesis.

Indirect hereditariness is a term we would apply to that departure from the healthy standard which may be traced to conditions not involving ill health on the part of the parents, but still known to induce a low state of vitality in their offspring. We receive some remarkable illustrations bearing upon the influence exerted by parents upon their progeny at the time of conception, when there is no question of the existence of disease, from a study of the brute creation. Our readers will readily recall the account given in the 30th chapter of Genesis, of the process adopted by Jacob* to ensure the production of lambs of a certain colour; and although we have no scientific data to establish the exact analogue in man, there can be little doubt that the fundamental law involved applies to him as well as to the lower creation. When we consider the persistence of impressions once made upon the tissues during extrauterine life, as shown, for instance, in the perpetuation of scars, where the abnormal cell-formation once produced repeats itself in every fresh layer of cell-growth, we need not be surprised at a reappearance of influences exerted at one impregnation upon future similar events.† That a previous impregnation may exercise an influence on subsequent impregnations, is illustrated by the following fact: a seven-eighths

* "Jacob took him rods of green poplar, and of the hazel and chestnut tree; and pilled white strakes on them, and made the white appear which was in the rods. And he set the rods which he had pilled before the flocks in the gutters in the watering troughs when the flocks came to drink, that they should conceive when they came to drink. And the flocks conceived before the rods, and brought forth cattle ringstraked, speckled, and spotted. And Jacob did separate the lambs, and set the faces of the flocks toward the ringstraked, and all the brown in the flock of Laban; and he put his own flocks by themselves, and put them not unto Laban's cattle. And it came to pass, whensoever the stronger cattle did conceive, that Jacob laid the rods before the eyes of the cattle in the gutters, that they might conceive among the rods. But when the cattle were feeble, he put them not in: so the feebler were Laban's, and the stronger Jacob's."

† See British and Foreign Medical Review, July 1846, p. 142.

Arabian mare, belonging to the Earl of Morton, had her first foal by a quagga; subsequently she had three other foals by a black Arabian. Now, the first two foals of these three by the Arabian had a striking resemblance to the quagga in the markings of their coat and in the form of their mane. It is necessarily difficult, if not morally impossible, to adduce similar illustrations of the law of transmission of qualities in the Anglo-Saxon race; but when we refer to the results exhibited in the intercourse between white and dark races of man, we meet with evidence of a satisfactory character, showing that impressions are perpetuated at the time of conception.

Common observation has long established the fact that qualities found in one generation are transmissible, per saltum, to the second generation in descent, or traceable upwards in the same way; * so that, in regard to life insurance, the relation between grandparents and grandchildren may become a question of importance. The predominant influence exerted by one or other parent, though difficult to formularise with precision, is also constantly manifested in the greater resemblance in future, in character and in constitutional peculiarity, of the offspring to either father or mother. Therefore, in cases of doubt as to the existence of any special proclivity on the part of an individual, his resemblance to either of his progenitors may assist in guiding the judgment. There are several factors to be considered here—the previous

* This peculiarity in the law of hereditary transmission has been termed Atavism.

health of the parents,* their special condition † at the time of sexual intercourse, the condition of the mother during utero-gestation; but we should be led away from the practical purpose of this book if we were to go into details, which, in the present state of science, must necessarily be more or less speculative.

There are, however, two points in the relations of the parents which are of undoubted influence upon their children, and which have been removed by direct observation from the domain of hypothesis. We allude to the influence upon the offspring depending upon great disparity of age between father and mother, and upon their consanguinity.

The procreative powers arrive at maturity at the period of puberty, which varies somewhat in different climates, but is always earlier in the female than in the male. The vigour of the offspring depends closely upon the vigour of the parents; it is not, therefore,

* Many curious facts and observations bearing upon this point are to be found in Walker's work on Intermarriage, (London, 1838). Thus we are informed that, "if a stallion be prevented, even by accidental lameness, from obtaining exercise, he is sure to be deficient in muscular power, and to convey that deficiency to his offspring. I knew a horse who broke his leg when running a race when three years old, and who has since been kept for covering mares, not being capable of anything else, or even of travelling for that; but his stock are not promising, though he is exceedingly well bred." See also, On the Transmission from Parent to Offspring of some Forms of Disease, by James Whitehead, M.D. London, 1857.

† The experience of the reader will probably supply him with instances corroborative of the influence hinted at, and of which that profound observer of nature, the poet Gœthe, avails himself to give point to his remarkable psychological novel, Die Wahlverwandschaften.

physiologically desirable that very early marriages should be encouraged. There is comparatively little danger of men marrying too early, as in the bulk of the population in our country the cost of living and the labour necessary to insure an income adequate to support a wife, proves a sufficient bar to excessive haste. The danger is rather on the side of the female, where attractions too often are a cause of wiser considerations being set aside, and the young woman, dazzled by the will-o'-the-wisp of independence, is tempted, before her frame is well knit and she is sufficiently developed in all her organs, to undergo the revolutionary changes which marriage entails upon her system.

What wonder that the girl of 17 or 18, whose bones are only half consolidated, and whose pelvis, especially, with its muscular and ligamentous surroundings, is yet far from maturity, loses her health after marriage, and becomes the delicate mother of sickly children? Parents who have the real interest and happiness of their daughters at heart, ought, in consonance with the laws of physiology, to discountenance marriage before 20; and the nearer the girls arrive at the age of 25 before the consummation of this important rite, the greater the probability that physically and morally they will be protected against those risks which precocious* marriages bring in their train.

There scarcely appears to be any natural

* "Les mariages trop précoces amènent la stérilité et produisent des enfans qui ont moins de probabilité de vivre."—Quetelet, Sur l'Homme, vol. i. p. 65.

limit to the procreative powers of man after puberty;* the sexual powers are often reduced and annulled at an early age by excesses or by disease, but there are many instances on record of healthy men having become fathers at a period of life when their female contemporaries would have passed the reproductive age by several decennia. When a man in advanced life takes a partner, he too often allows himself to be led away from the paths of prudence by youth and beauty; and we then find not only that the father often pays a penalty to which it is not now our province to allude, but that his offspring exhibit physical defects, which manifest themselves in a variety of ways, but always tend more or less to diminish its vital power and its prospects of longevity. Hence one point to be considered in life insurance is the relative age of the candidate's parents at the time of his birth. As the average age at marriage in England is 25, the influence we have just discussed does not very often present itself for our consideration, but where it occurs it should not be overlooked.

The Mosaic law, which in so many points harmonises with the most recent developments of natural science, dwells most wisely on the question of consanguinity in marriage. It is one of such

* Thomas Parr of Winnington, Shropshire, who died 1635, aged 152, married at the age of 80 for the first time, and lived with his wife for 32 years, but during her lifetime and when 105 years old, he had an illegitimate child by Catherine Milton, for which he did penance in Alderbury Church. After the death of his first wife, he married again at the age of 122, and had one child.—Records of Longevity, by Thos. Bailey: London, 1857, p. 291.

importance at the present day, that one might almost be tempted to regard it as an argument against the original unity of the race. Be that as it may, it is irrefragable that intermarriages among relations is most prejudicial upon the resulting progeny. Frequently they are barren, and that is the issue that, under the circumstances, might be desired for all; for general debility, defects in vital organs, and especially in the nervous centres, and a special perpetuation of those vices of conformation that pre-exist in the parents, are the almost invariable result. If our divines, instead of squabbling over a canonical law prohibiting the widower from marrying his deceased wife's sister, would study physiology as bearing upon the laws of reproduction, they would probably arrive at the conclusion, that while they might safely leave the former question to be dealt with at the discretion of the persons immediately concerned, they would do a wise thing to obtain an enactment forbidding the marriage of cousins of the first and second degree. That sterility is a frequent present penalty upon the intermarriage of relatives, is confirmed by the fact that when one partner dies and the survivor marries a person with whom there is no trace of blood relationship, healthy children are born. The general law appears to be that, the more fresh blood is introduced into a family or race, the more vigorous the descendants are likely to be.

Provided there be none of the accidental deviations from natural law to which we have alluded in the foregoing pages, we may assume it proven that healthy progenitors are followed by healthy descendants.

We shall now consider the special influences and proclivities of a morbid type, which tend to reproduce themselves by hereditary transmission, and which merit a special study by all medical men; in regard to their influence on longevity as connected with life assurance they deserve particular attention. The whole subject of the diathesis, or predisposition to special diseases, is bound up with this question. We have to deal with an impress transmitted from father to son, and from grandfather to grandson, which may or may not be manifested at birth, but is likely to appear under favouring conditions at any later period of existence, according to the peculiar character of the taint. Here again the predominant influence of one or other parent at the time of sexual intercourse exercises a palpable effect upon the offspring, otherwise it seems impossible to account for the escape of some members of the same family from an influence to which all appear to have been equally subject. Physical training and care may do much to neutralise the hereditary taint, but it is a question whether it can be entirely obliterated in one generation. There is probably no limit to the possible reproduction of morbid conditions of tissue and structure, nor can we determine the range of influence exerted upon the embryo and fœtus during intra-uterine life, apart from the impress communicated by the paternal parent; but for the purpose we have in view, we may limit our consideration to certain well-marked features in the transmission of morbid peculiarities.* Syphilis, scrofula, tubercle,

* The reader will find some useful hints on this subject in

cancer, gout, rheumatism, epilepsy, and insanity, with their allies and derivatives, are the fell names that here come into prominence.

Whatever hereditary diseases appear in a well-marked form, the observer will not fail to recognise them and estimate their bearing upon the longevity of the individual. But in connection with life assurance, we have to deal ordinarily with a person professing to be in good health, and in whom the faintest indication of a taint must be sought for in order to establish its influence upon his constitution and upon accidental diseases that may arise. The hereditary taint of syphilis has long been a subject of earnest discussion among medical men, and modern research has traced numerous lesions of vital organs to its influence, though these, in the adult, are probably more often due to the remarkable latency of the poison for long years after primary infection. In many cases the effect of scrofula and some forms of inveterate syphilis resemble one another so closely as to have caused them to be regarded as identical by authors of eminence. Mr. Whitehead,* who has paid much attention to this subject, views sycosis as a congener of syphilis, upon which he has found it supervene, while he has seen phenomena simulating lues venerea occurring in the offspring of one affected with sycosis. It is not improbable that, with the advance of chemistry and microscopy, we may be able to recognise the existence of this and

Dr. Copland's Dictionary of Medicine, under the head of "Disease," vol. i. p. 556.

* Whitehead, on the Transmission from parent to offspring of some forms of Disease, p. 66.

other taints through direct evidence obtainable by an examination of the tissues, and especially of the blood. Dr. Garrod, Dr. Sanderson, and others, have already done much in this direction, but we are yet far from having attained to a reliable method of recognising the diathesis, the indirect or circumstantial evidence being generally all that we have to build our conclusions upon. Whether, in certain cases, scrofulous and venereal affections are identical or not, there can be no doubt that the scrofulous diathesis possesses in a marked manner the attributes of an hereditary malady. The glandular enlargements that characterise scrofula may very commonly be traced as belonging to several generations of the same family; just as the tumid lips, high cheek-bones, fair hair and complexion, broad alæ nasi, irregular digestion, and general want of tone, regarded as features characteristic of the scrofulous type, recur again and again in members of the same stock.* The scrofulous individual is more liable to developing any accidental diseases which attack him, into dangerous forms, and to be prostrated by them, than a person in whom no such predisposition exists. The former is less able to bear the shocks and trials of life to which humanity is unavoidably exposed than the latter; cæteris paribus therefore, he is less eligible for life insurance.

We need not here discuss the question of identity or non-identity of scrofula and tubercle. We confess ourselves as adherents of the non-identity doc-

* See Scrofula; its Nature, Causes, etc., by Benjamin Phillips, F.R.S. London, 1846.

trine, both on the ground of personal observation and study. But that a correlation between them, and furthermore with syphilis, exists can scarcely be denied by the advocates of either view. Certainly in none of the three is the hereditary character more palpably displayed than in tubercle or phthisis. Upon the general fact all writers are agreed, but they differ as to the exact frequency of this influence, owing to the different manner in which they have carried out their researches. The authorities of the Brompton Hospital for consumption inform us that they find an hereditary tendency in 246 out of 1010 cases, or in 24.35 per cent; but this result is too favourable, unless we limit our inquiry to the antecedents of a patient's parents. Dr. Fuller * has shown that if the existence of the disease in either grandparent be considered as evidence of the transmission of the disease to the grandchildren, a proposition which has our entire assent, the proportion will rise to 43.6 per cent; and if the predisposing influence exhibited by death of uncles and aunts from consumption be included in the calculation, the proportion will rise to 59.5 per cent.

We would go even further. For our experience has convinced us that we derive as important indications from an examination of the history of collaterals, as of ascending generations. In this we are borne out by the elaborate investigations of Dr. Theodore Williams.† He finds that the number of

* On Diseases of the Chest, by H. W. Fuller, M.D. London, 1862, p. 348.

† On the Duration of Phthisis Pulmonalis, by C. T. Williams, M.D.—*Med.-Chir. Trans.*, vol. liv. p. 95.

cases of consumption having only brothers and sisters affected with that disease constitutes a percentage of 46 per cent—a percentage which, as will appear from the following table, is larger than that of any other class of relations. Of a total of 484

10 had grandparents affected.
43 had fathers affected.
67 had mothers affected.
10 had both parents affected.
48 had uncles and aunts affected.
72 had father's or mother's family affected (particulars unknown).
224 had brothers and sisters affected.
10 had cousins affected.

Dr. Theodore Williams' analysis of cases also demonstrates that the family predisposition shows itself more in the females of a family than in the males, the difference amounting to 14 per cent; while they confirm the prevailing opinion, which is commonly acted upon in determining the relative increase of life assurance rates, that the presence of phthisis in mothers has a greater influence upon the recurrence of the disease in their children, than its presence in the fathers, to the extent of nearly 5 per cent.

The phthisical taint shows itself in other ways than in the occurrence of tubercular disease. It appears to generate a special liability to disease of the mucous membranes; hence the prevalence in phthisical families of bronchitis and pleuro-pneumonia, the antecedence of which, in an applicant for insurance, receives greater or less significance according to the force of collateral evidence as to his immunity or the reverse, from the debilitating conditions involved in an hereditary proclivity.

The proclivity to phthisis commences at puberty, and though the succeeding ten years are generally regarded as the most fertile period of life for the development of this disease, this view is based upon a fallacy, as the disease is statistically shown to occur with almost uniform frequency up to the decline of life. After 50, the proportion of deaths from phthisis to those living is nearly the same as at an earlier period. This is particularly important in regard to life insurance, as it warns us not to disregard the hereditary influences in any person offering to insure, whatever the age. In childhood, the tubercular predisposition, for reasons which it does not concern us to dwell upon, shows itself rather in the brain and abdomen than in the pulmonary tissue, and this has to be borne in mind in estimating the indications afforded by collaterals as to hereditary taint.

Supposing we have a candidate for insurance before us who presents an unexceptionable personal history, how are we to rate various influences of an hereditary character connected with the disease in question? It seems a fair rule to add seven years where a father, and ten where the mother is shown to have been consumptive. The usage of offices is, we believe, to disregard the death of one collateral from phthisis; we question whether this is in accordance with the evidence we have adduced. Certainly, where two of the same generation have succumbed to the disease, an addition of 7 or 10 years is necessary. If both the parents have died consumptive, hazardous rates of 20 or 25 years only can be admitted, and it is a question whether such lines ought not to be absolutely rejected. Wherever there is a doubt as to the interpretation of a candidate's history, as when pulmonary disease under another name appears rife in a family, the medical officer ought to give the company the benefit of the doubt, and recommend increased rates or the rejection of the life. A great deal passes under the name of bronchitis and pneumonia and "child-birth," which is really tubercle; the duration of the attack, and the accompanying circumstances, will often aid in arriving at a correct conclusion. The existence of any symptoms of phthisis, in a candidate whose family history is doubtful, makes a rejection of course imperative, but to this question we shall have occasion to refer more in detail later on.

Authorities differ as to the frequency with which cancer is hereditary, but all are agreed as to the general fact. From the suffering it so frequently entails, it attracts perhaps even more attention than tubercular disease, but it is very much less frequent; for while, according to the latest Report of the Registrar-General for 1871, there are close upon 70,000 deaths from tubercular disease in England, divided almost equally between males and females, there are under 10,000 deaths from cancer, of which 6631 occurred in females, and less than half that number, or 3060, in males. Velpeau was of opinion that 1 in 3 cases of cancer showed a hereditary taint; Sir James Paget's investigations yielded 1 in 4; Mr. Sibley concluded from the statistics of Middlesex Hospital that the proportion was nearly 1 in 12. Practically we cannot ignore the undoubted hereditariness of cancer, and as the female organs of reproduction are specially liable to the disease, and we have seen that the female sex has an infinitely greater proclivity to cancer generally than the male sex, we must specially consider the influence of this hereditary taint where we have to deal with a female applicant for insurance. Cancer is a disease *per se*, and is commonly found to exclude tubercle; but undoubtedly the two may co-exist in the same individual;* and where both occur in the same family, any member of it must be regarded as bearing a double risk, that should be proportionately taxed if he be at all admissible.

Rheumatism is another form of disease, the tendency to which is hereditary in an undeniable manner. It is not so directly fatal as the maladies we have recently considered, but it contributes largely, in an indirect manner, by impairing vital power and damaging the heart, towards swelling the lists of mortality. Dr. Fuller † found that of 246 patients admitted into St. George's Hospital with acute rheumatism, 71, or 28·8 per cent, showed an hereditary predisposition to the disease from its having occurred in one or other parent. He is borne out in this view by the observations of Chomel, Macleod, and other physicians of eminence.

Gout, again, which largely impairs life, is, like rheumatism, undoubtedly hereditary, and has long

* See on this point some observations and cases given by Mr. Weeden Cooke in his work on Cancer, its Allies and Counterfeits. London, 1865, p. 11, and *sqq.*

† On Rheumatism, etc., p. 32.

been recognised as possessing this character; it is one of those heirlooms that people are even disposed to boast of, on account of a certain air of respectability that attaches to family gout. Here, thanks to the labours of Dr. Garrod,* more than in any other so-called blood-diseases, we have direct evidence of the existence of an abnormal constituent in the blood, leading us to hope that the same line of research to which Dr. Sanderson and other men of eminence in this country and abroad are devoting their attention may eventuate in a more ready recognition of the poison or anomaly that underlies most diathetic conditions. Dr. Garrod confirms the results arrived at by Sir C. Scudamore's analysis of 522 cases, showing the hereditary influence to prevail in more than one-half. But the gouty diathesis exhibits itself in many patients in whom a bona fide attack of gout has never occurred, in degenerative conditions of the heart, blood-vessels, and secernent organs, as well as in the nervous system, which must not be lost sight of by a medical examiner for insurance. A great deal must be left to his individual judgment and experience, as, although it is usual to take off three years from the expectation of life of a person who is shown to have had gout, we have not sufficiently precise data to estimate the hereditary influence in those who escape the regular paroxysm, but are found to possess indications of impaired vitality derived from gouty predecessors.

The hereditary taint shows itself in a marked

* The Nature and Treatment of Gout, by A. B. Garrod, M.D., F.R.S. London, 1859.

manner in the various diseases referable to the nerve-centres, but more in those which are connected with the brain than with the spinal cord. They are, however, with certain exceptions, chiefly the appanage of advanced life, and do not affect life insurance by any means in the same ratio as diseases of the thoracic and abdominal viscera. Thus apoplexy is most common between 60 and 70. Dr. Begbie's* Analysis of the Mortality of the Scottish Widows' Fund for 30 years shows that of 72 cases 20 deaths occurred before and 52 after the age of sixty, whereas among 72 cases of phthisis 35 deaths occurred between 30 and 40. The hereditary taint often shows itself in the reproduction of brain-disease of a different form from that in which it appeared in the ancestors—a marked correlation existing between apoplexy and its ally paralysis, epilepsy, hysteria, asthma, and insanity. Epilepsy, which unfortunately occurs most frequently in early life, exhibits in a marked form the hereditary impress, as well as this correlation; though, like most other diseases, it may arise spontaneously from purely idiopathic causes. Insanity, again, belongs to the morbid conditions in which the hereditary influence is strongly marked, though it does not appear largely to affect life insurance business. Doctors Bucknill and Tuke† tell us that, though acute insanity shortens life materially, the chronic form does not exhibit that tendency. Dr. Wood even found that of 46 incurable

* Monthly Journal of Medical Science, January 1847.

† A Manual of Psychological Medicine, by J. C. Buckmill, M.D., and D. A. Tuke, M.D. London, 1858, p. 268.

patients at Bethlehem the average duration of life somewhat exceeded that of an equal number of lives among the sane of good health. Taking the statistics of insanity on an extended scale, however, there is no doubt that the general mortality of insane persons is larger than that of the sane; for though it varies in the different asylums from 5·06 to 19·1 per cent, even the lowest average is considerably above the general mortality of the population, which, in 1871, was 2·22 per cent. The hereditary influence is admitted by all writers on the subject, both British and foreign; and it is asserted that it is especially observed among those classes of the community, as among Jews and Quakers, who usually intermarry in their own fraternity. It also appears that the hereditary taint is more frequently met with in the higher than in the lower classes,* as Esquirol,† for instance, met with 152 out of 264 cases in his private practice, whereas Sir William Ellis ‡ discovered an inherited influence only in 214 cases out of 1380, at the Middlesex Pauper Lunatic Asylum.

Many speculative questions suggest themselves with reference to inherited influences beyond what has been alluded to. But our wish is to keep as much as possible on the path of established or approximately established fact; and therefore we

* This may be partly attributable to the greater strain on the mind to which numbers of the upper classes of society are subjected, in which the high pressure of modern life has a tendency to foster brain-disorders of all kinds.

† Dictionnaire des Sciences Médicales, tomes xvi. and xxx.

‡ Reports of Hanwell, 1839.

avoid mere hypothesis, which should, though not altogether to be set aside, be as little as possible countenanced in matters of life insurance. There is not an organ or part of the body in which peculiarities of function or tissue are not frequently traceable in the ascending or descending line; and it is always well for the medical man to bear in mind this general law of transmissibility, and to estimate the special bearing of any recurrent deviation from the normal condition. Heart-disease, disease of the chylopoietic viscera, as shown in various forms of dyspepsia, and especially in diabetes, renal affections, and diseases of the veins, are among those disorders for which the practitioner not unfrequently discovers an hereditary origin. But we do not possess sufficiently precise data to put statistical proofs of the frequency of this predisposition before our readers, and must be content with the general indication, leaving to each medical man the application to every individual instance.

We have alluded above to the possibility of obtaining information on the subject of hereditary transmission by arguing back from the children to their parents. If it be true that healthy parents bring forth healthy children, it appears to follow that an unhealthy progeny argues a vitiated stock. And so it certainly does; but this element, though of much importance to the political economist or anthropologist, is only of minor consideration to the insurance physician, because the great majority of persons who insure their lives do so either before they have a family or when it is rather in *posse* than in *esse*. We would, however, take this opportunity of entering our protest against the prevailing habit of treating the deaths of young children too much as a matter of course, either as an inscrutable act of Providence, or as a providential arrangement to prevent over-population. We believe neither in the necessity of premature death nor of disease; and though neglect and ignorance of natural laws that rule the training of the infant bear a large share in the mortality of young children, we dare not shut our eyes to the fact that premature decay is very often the result of a taint imparted to them by their parents; when this is capable of satisfactory proof it is manifest that, according to its specific character, it must reduce, to employ life insurance phraseology, the value of the lives of the latter.

CHAPTER V.

THE HISTORY OF THE INDIVIDUAL.

We now proceed to examine those points in the personal history of the candidate for insurance which are to guide us in forming an opinion as to his eligibility, in gauging the deteriorating influences to which he may have been subjected, or in advising the company to reject the life altogether as uninsurable. The medical officer has a responsible duty to perform. Two parties are both desirous of entering into a contract, and he is eventually the person who determines the basis of the contract. The company is desirous, on the one hand, of doing business; but if it is well conducted, it does not wish to risk its stability by laxity in selecting the lives, or to incur the imputation of too great and unreasonable severity in rejecting them on inadequate grounds. On the other hand, the person who has made up his mind to take out a policy, has a right to fair treatment, as an unnecessary increase of premium touches his pocket at once, and rejection not only prevents his making the desired provision for his family at one office, but renders him, owing to the mutual understanding that exists between all first-class offices, less liable to be accepted elsewhere; besides seriously affecting his morale, by informing him that he has small chance of attaining to the average term of life, of which he may have had no previous suspicion. If he is sufficiently trained for his work, and performs his task without fear or favour, the medical officer, like any man who does his duty, may act without fear of consequences; but incapacity or hasty judgment will certainly before long recoil upon him in this relation as in every other.

The general aspect of the examinee is probably the first point that will attract the examiner's attention; who will notice the gait, the manner, the speech, the complexion; and bear in mind any peculiarity that may be an indication of previous habits, for comparison with the applicant's statements. If the first impression is ever so favourable, the applicant's age corresponds with his appearance, and no flaw is to be detected in the reports of his friends or in his own statement, a personal inquiry into the different points bearing upon the duration of life still is necessary; because, without an intentional fraud, there will be a natural bias to adopt a favourable interpretation, and a fair exterior may hide internal mischief; just as accidental circumstances may mislead the examiner into the belief in a morbid taint, where a careful examination fails to detect anything of the kind.

We have already shown that occupation has a marked bearing on longevity, an hereditary or personal defect, that may merit no attention under certain circumstances, may become the subject of grave suspicion in others. An occasional attack of simple catarrh or bronchitis would not justify an increased rate in a professional man or a merchant; whereas in the baker, who is exposed to great vicissitudes of temperature, to the inhalation of flour and dust, and who is deprived of the normal allowance of sleep, the danger of the affection merging into consumption, or other serious lung disease, would operate very differently. A commercial traveller is exposed to the double risk entailed by constant railway travelling, and to social claims that exist among his fraternity, which is necessarily increased if his particular specialty requires him to be on intimate terms with the bar, and he has to recommend the produce of fermentation and distillation. Continuous railway travelling, apart from the direct injury resulting from accidents, is prejudicial in various ways ; and many persons who reside at a distance from their place of business, in order to benefit by country or sea air, neutralise these advantages by the wear and tear to body and mind incidental to daily railway journeys, even if the distance is not considerable.* Many is the time when, on medical grounds, we have seen reason to discountenance such an arrangement ; and where, as in underground railways, the passenger, during his transit from the breakfast-table to a dingy office, or back again, is further deprived of the influence of fresh air and exercise morning and evening, which he might have by walking or driving the same distance, with more distraction, the objection becomes still greater. From the involuntary efforts constantly made during the quick transit to preserve the equilibrium of the body, a peculiar burden is laid upon the muscular system, while the constant succussion that the body is subjected to overtaxes the nervous system, and is

* See on the subject of railway travelling, *The Lancet*, Jan. 11, 1862.

conducive to paralytic affections; again, the rapid succession of objects, the noises, the necessity for being constantly on the alert, affects the brain through the eye and the ear, while it excites both the respiratory and circulatory systems. It is found that members of the post-office staff are frequently incapacitated from acting in the travelling service by the prejudicial influence of railway locomotion, and that "bilious" persons are particularly unsuited for that kind of work. In no way can railway travelling be regarded as conducive to health; and if we have to deal with a person who cannot avoid spending much of his time in trains, this may influence the rate to be demanded, especially if any suspicion of brain-disease, or a tendency to it, already exists.

The following table, which we extract from the *Lancet*, and which shows the number of days during which the members of each class are laid up by sickness, exhibits strikingly the influence of railway travelling upon health:—

Age.	England and Wales at large.	Heavy Labor.		Mariners.	Railway Officials.
		Without Exposure.	With Exposure.		
20	26·62	26·47	28·69	16·89	31·00
25	23·94	25·10	26·47	15·61	33·06
30	22·57	23·45	25·74	17·96	33·94
35	22·38	24·00	25·64	18·86	34·11
40	23·26	24·34	27·01	17·89	32.23
45	24·11	25·14	28·14	20·51	32·10
50	26·00	28·10	29·34	22·27	30·43
60	31·07	33·25	35·42	28·00	41·76

Among the dangerous trades are to be classed those which are exposed to the inhalation of dust. This is one of the causes inducing a large mortality among bakers, miners, and cotton operatives, but especially among the steel-grinders of Sheffield. Dr. Holland of that town has especially drawn attention to the causes of the maladies from which they suffer and the circumstances under which they work. The grinders' asthma, which has been traced to the inhalation of particles of steel, gives rise to irritation of the pulmonary tissues, inducing a form of consumption of the most intractable nature, so that few of this class of operatives survive the age of 35. Other influences are also undoubtedly at work to cause this high rate of mortality ; but as the Sheffield grinder rarely becomes a candidate for life insurance, we need not dwell upon his habits in this place. The same applies to the working stone mason, who, owing to the inhalation of stone dust, suffers similarly, though in a minor degree. The fact of his operations being conducted more in the open air is in his favour ; and this leads us to remark generally of all trades, that the more they involve confinement in a close atmosphere, a cramped posture, and a temptation to drink, the greater the liability to receive or develop any taint to which they are exposed. It is rare that we have to deal with one element only in the causation of disease.

Thus the printer presents a very unfavourable mortality, owing to the ill-ventilated, small, overcrowded apartments, often only lit with gas, in which he works. The depression thus induced leads to a large consumption of alcoholic beverages, which further charge his blood with deleterious compounds, and the handling of the types, composed of antimony and lead, induces the direct poisoning that leads to paralytic and convulsive diseases.

Here, as in most trades, improvements are constantly being effected, and it is not too much to hope that as sanitary science becomes more and more diffused, the progress that has already taken place will eventuate in removing all those causes of excessive mortality which have been recognised and are under the control of man.

The trade of the painter and plumber, from their being subjected to the influence of salts of lead, often gives rise to paralytic conditions, and to impaired nutrition of the heart, and induces a proclivity to gout.* This is due to the absorption of lead † into the system, which may be guarded against by using certain precautions, of which cleanliness is the chief; but it is found that an undue proportion of deaths also occur in these trades from accident. The classes of men that are worst off in this respect are seamen, miners, and engine drivers, for whom it is the com-

* Garrod on Gout, p. 282. See also, at p. 284, Dr. Christison's remarkable statement as to the immunity of the printers in Edinburgh, and the reasons assigned by him.

† The general population also frequently present instances of lead-poisoning through the introduction of the salts of the metal by the lungs or the stomach. Thus it has occurred through wine sweetened by litharge, water that has dissolved a salt of lead when contained in leaden pipes or cisterns, cider, rum, and sugar impregnated with the deleterious metal. Snuff has repeatedly been known to cause serious and even fatal effects from being adulterated with salts of lead.

mon practice to charge a special rate on account of the risk their occupation brings with it, amounting to from 15s. to 40s. per cent on the average premium for healthy lives. The extra rate for mariners is generally 25s. per cent per annum, that for miners 20s., and a little less for mining engineers and agents. Mr. Harben* gives their relative mortality from accident as follows:—

Seamen	35 per cent.
Miners and quarrymen	25 „ „
Engine attendants	15 „ „
Painters, plumbers, and glaziers . . .	10 „ „

We may quote from the same authority one or two other facts connected with the question of violent deaths, for which we should scarcely have been prepared. Mr. Harben tells us that more deaths from violence occur in males from 10 to 19 years than at any other age; that from 20 to 39 more married men die from that cause than bachelors; but that at 40 years and upwards, single males and females die in greater proportion from violence than those who have entered into a matrimonial partnership. These statistics suggest some curious psychological and physiological problems, which, however, this is not the place to discuss. We have already seen that the highest rate of mortality is found among inn and beer-shop keepers. It is difficult to determine why in civil life butchers rank next to them, because their occupation is not in itself to be considered unhealthy, nor one ordinarily entailing much anxiety. In both, probably,

* Mortality Experience of the Prudential Assurance Company, by Henry Harben. London, 1871.

the danger arises from the temptations they are subjected to of indulging in habitual dram-drinking. The publican is constantly surrounded by an atmosphere of alcohol; and few of his class escape the train of symptoms indicating successively disorder of the stomach, the liver, the kidneys, and the brain, which this insidious poison excites and fosters with fatal pertinacity.

The practice of insurance companies with regard to publicans varies; some, we believe, exclude them altogether. This we regard as harsh and unnecessary, and scarcely compatible with the philanthropic spirit which underlies insurance business. On the other hand, we consider the ordinary addition of 10 per cent as far too low for this very hazardous trade, and should consider five-and-twenty per cent more in accordance with what is just, until the devoutly-to-be-wished-for consummation of a marked improvement in the vital statistics of publicans can be demonstrated.

But, unfortunately, in all classes of the community the abuse of alcoholic beverages prevails to a large extent,* and the inquiry into the amount taken by the individual is always fraught with difficulty. The spirit-drinkers of every class are liable to suspicion, but wherever it is elicited that ardent spirits in any form are habitually or frequently taken during the

* Mr. Neison's calculations give—

1 drunkard to every 74 of the male population.
1 " " 434 of the female population.
1 " " 145 of both sexes above the age of 20.

We fear that more recent investigations show even a larger proportion.

day, the suspicion amounts to a certainty that the life, in insurance parlance, may be considered as a damaged one.

Mr. Neison,* in a very elaborate paper on the rate of mortality among persons of intemperate habits, shows that the expectation of life of intemperate persons is much below the average; and that an intemperate person of 20 has reduced the average expectation from 44·2 years to 15·6; a person of 30, from 36·5 to 13·8 years; a person at the age of 40, from 28·8 to 11·6 years; and also that while diseases of the nervous system and digestive organs give rise to 15·9 per cent of deaths in the population at large, they form 50·40 per cent of all deaths among the intemperate.

Intemperance reduces the expectation of life more in the upper classes than among mechanics and tradesmen.

Mr. Neison finds that from the age of 16 upwards the relative mortality of intemperate persons exceeds that of the general population of England 3·25 times. At the term of life 21 to 30 the mortality is upwards of five times that of the general community, and in the succeeding 20 years of life it is above four times greater. He offers the consolatory remark that the drinking practices of society have improved during the last quarter of a century, and that what (in 1851) was commonly regarded as free living,

* Journal of the Statistical Society, Sept. 1851, vol. xiv. A valuable paper on the same subject is also published by Mr. Scratchley in his Contributions to Vital Statistics: London, 1857, p. 201.

would some years since only have been regarded as moderation. "In like manner," he adds, "it may be hoped that the usages of society will continue to improve; and, at no distant date, the habits now considered not to exceed the bounds of moderation be altogether unknown in polite and refined society."

The following table, taken from Mr. Neison's essay, exhibits in a striking manner the relative mortality of intemperate and temperate individuals, and justifies the startling conclusions arrived at by Mr. Neison, while it shows the special proclivity of certain organs to suffer under the pernicious influence of alcoholic beverages:—

RATIO PER CENT OF DEATHS AT AGES 20 AND UPWARD FROM DIFFERENT CAUSES, TO THE TOTAL DEATHS FROM ALL CAUSES AT THE CORRESPONDING AGES IN THE GENERAL COMMUNITY.

Causes of Death.	England and Wales 1847.	Gotha Life Office.	Scottish Widows' Fund.	*Intemperate Lives.*
Head Diseases .	9·710	15·176	20·720	27·10
Digestive Organs	6·240	8·377	11·994	23·30
Respiratory . .	33·150	27·843	23·676	22·98
Total	49·100	51·396	56·390	73·38

This table indicates the true bearing of intemperance, not so much in being itself the immediate cause of death as in its increasing the fatality of other disease; were this not the case, the small number of deaths set down to alcoholism and delirium tremens combined (for both sexes it amounted in 1871 only to 740) would scarcely attract attention, and the subject would not merit all the space we have bestowed upon it. The freedom from intoxication and the baneful effects of chronic alcoholism in countries where the primary products of fermentation of grape juice are used by the population, and our experience in our own country to the same purport,* makes it impossible for the medical man to condemn the moderate use of wine, and we equally question whether deleterious effects can ordinarily be traced to unadulterated malt liquors. Even where abuse can be shown, this would be as little an argument in favour of general teetotalism as if some one were to assert that, because the greater part of London, Hamburg, and Chicago were destroyed by fire, we were to be debarred the use of fire to cook our meals. Though we highly honour those who, from conscientious motives and for the supposed good of their fellows, take the pledge of total abstinence from all fermented liquors, we think that a higher morality, as well as better knowledge, displays itself in avoiding their baneful abuse and encouraging their wholesome employment. Unfortunately for the cause of teetotalism, its advocates have scarcely as yet given satisfactory proof that their system possesses all the advantages they claim for it. Mr. Scratchley,† after exhibiting

* The special injury resulting from ardent spirits, as compared with the produce of the primary fermentation of the grape and of malt, is also shown in the statistical paper of Mr. Neison just quoted.

† Contributions to Vital Statistics, p. 218.

the striking effects which intemperance exerts upon longevity, goes on to remark—" It would be curious to contrast with the above results the rate of mortality among persons who have been for a considerable period of years, or for the whole of life, abstainers from intoxicating drinks ; but, unfortunately, there are no available data connected with this class of lives, and it seems there will long be considerable difficulty in procuring such information. A few years ago Mr. Munro of Enfield, at much trouble and expense, procured returns from Rechabite societies, showing the rate of mortality and sickness experienced by the members ; and it is known that the results, although not published, exhibit as high a rate of mortality and sickness as is found to prevail among the members of other friendly societies. The facts collected by Mr. Munro are of great value, and it is to be regretted that the societies furnishing them should, on account of the unfavourable nature of the results arrived at, object to their publication." Mr. Scratchley seeks to offer the Rechabites a little comfort under these unfavourable circumstances, for he goes on to say that " although they show a high rate of mortality, it should be kept in view that all the members cannot be considered as the type of total abstainers, many of them being reformed drunkards, and, as such, have become teetotallers with broken-down constitutions. " The author, therefore, infers that " until Rechabite societies have enrolled a class of members who have been abstainers from infancy, they cannot expect an entire immunity from those diseases and deteriorating influences to which less careful members of the community are subject." It is, however, only fair to state that since this was written, Mr. Samuel Brown has stated that the temperance section of the Temperance Provident Life Office exhibited a lower rate of mortality than the general section. Milton anticipated this controversy, and concentrated the pith of the matter in the following exquisite lines:—

> "If all the world
> Should, in a fit of temp'rance, feed on pulse,
> Drink the clear stream, and nothing wear but frieze,
> Th' Allgiver would be unthank'd, would be unprais'd,
> Not half his riches known, and yet despis'd."

In the present state of society it is, unfortunately, not only a question of quantity which determines the hurtful or harmless effect of alcoholic liquors, but we are surrounded by dangers, owing to the clever adulterations which are palmed upon us as genuine articles. Here science and the sanitary medical officer must be called in to protect us. As milk, the mildest and most wholesome of all beverages, may bring death and misery into families through the iniquity of the dairyman, so adulteration may render the most wholesome alcoholic beverages unfit for human consumption. The caveat-emptor principle is scarcely applicable, because the purchaser can have neither the knowledge nor the means of testing every glass that he drinks, and his taste is often so perverted that he learns to prefer the poisonous compounds to the healthy produce. It is here that legislative enactments are absolutely required of the most stringent character to prevent fraud, and to protect those who are unable to protect themselves.

We need not again dwell upon the value of professional lives, because we have already shown that they exhibit the highest averages. They are a practical illustration of the ancient saying, "in medio tutissimus ibis." We have also briefly adverted to the generally low average presented by crowned heads, which is of importance in regard to life insurance, not because they individually apply to be insured, but because, unknown to themselves, various life insurance contingencies are made to depend upon their lives. We are therefore tempted to say a few more words on the subject. The duration of life among the upper classes, according to Dr. Guy,* whose general conclusion agrees with those of Hufeland and Caspar on this point, varies inversely with their rank. Beginning with the class which has the shortest average duration of life, the several classes are found to stand in the following order:—

1. Sovereigns. 2. Male members of royal houses. 3. Female members of royal houses. 4. Peers, being successors to the title. 5. Male members of the peerage and baronetage. 6. Male members of the gentry. 7. Professional men. 8. Females of the upper classes. Hufeland tells us, that in the whole catalogue of Roman and German emperors, from Augustus downwards, amounting to 200, only four—Gordian, Valerius, Anastasius, and Justinian—attained the age of 80; while of 300 popes, only five reached that age. It appears, further, that in Germany the

* Journal of Statistical Society, vol. ix., 1846.

reigns of 38 emperors lasted on an average 19 years; in Sweden, 44 kings reigned 18 years each, in Russia 50 czars reigned on an average 15 years, while in our own country, bad as things have been, the average has been 22½ years.* A very elaborate article on the Duration of Life of Sovereigns is published by Dr. Guy in the tenth volume of the Journal of the Statistical Society, where the reader will find a variety of interesting information, the main inference from which is, that "whether we form an average from a large number of facts gleaned from a wide field of observation, or split up this single group into the smaller elements of which it consists, we arrive at the same conclusion, that sovereigns, as a class, are among the shortest-lived of human beings." In order to give further support to this statement, as well as on account of the general value of the table in reference to vital statistics, we extract from the same article the following figures, which Dr. Guy has compiled partly from his own researches and partly from those of Mr. Neison.

	Expectation of life at 30.
Agricultural Laborers (Benefit Societies)	40·6
Rural Districts do.	38·4
Town Districts do.	34·6
England (whole population)	34·1
Professions (chiefly clergy)	33·9
Assured Lives (Amicable)	33·7
City Districts (Benefit Societies)	32·9
English Gentry	31·2

* Quoted by Walford, p. 67, from Dr. Farr in M'Culloch's British Empire.

	Expectation of life at 30.
English Aristocracy . . .	30·9
Clerks (Benefit Societies) . . .	30·5
Liverpool do. . . .	30·1
Dundee (whole population) . .	29·1
Northampton Table (Price) . .	28·3
Sovereigns	27·3
Liverpool (whole population) . .	27·0
Glasgow do. . .	24·9

Our own Palmerston, and the distinguished statesman who has recently vacated the Presidential chair in France, are marked exceptions to the rule, that their order has the melancholy prerogative of falling early victims to the duties of their calling. The average duration of life of statesmen is only 56 years, while that of the professional classes is over 73.

Age.	Number of Deaths.					Per cent.				
	Roy. Houses		Aristocracy.	Gentry.	Females, Upper Classes.	Royal Houses.		Aristocracy.	Gentry.	Females, Upper Classes.
	Males	Fe-males				Males.	Fe-males.			
21-30	5	3	60	105	150	4·90	5·00	4·85	5·87	7·86
31-40	4	7	65	83	146	3·90	11·67	5·26	4·64	7·66
41-50	13	5	109	110	133	12·74	8·33	8·80	6·15	6·97
51-60	25	11	183	177	144	24·52	18·33	14·76	9·90	7·55
61-70	18	14	252	386	290	17·65	23·34	20·34	21·60	15·21
71-80	26	15	331	500	474	25·51	25·00	26·71	27·98	24·86
81-90	10	4	216	336	422	9·80	6·67	17·43	18·79	22·13
91-100 and upwards	1	1	23	90	148	0·96	1·67	1·85	5·07	7·76

The preceding table, given by Dr. Guy, affords a clearer survey of the mortality of the upper classes of this country than any paraphrastic statement that we could put before them; the numbers and percentage proportions are arranged in periods of 10 years.*

It is, however, only right to state, that Messrs. Bailey and Day question the correctness of the facts upon which Dr. Guy bases his calculations regarding the peerage, and their researches lead them to different results. They state that the average mean duration of male lives among the families of the peerage is, at all ages under 73, greater than that of the general population of the country, greater even than among the selected lives of the Equitable Society (with the unimportant exception of the period from 15 to 21), greater at all ages under 62 than among the Government annuitants, and throughout, approaches to the standard mortality of the healthy districts. With regard to female lives, these authors find that the mean duration in the peerage is throughout materially greater than with the general population, indicating a more favourable mortality at the older ages than any table with which they are acquainted. As with the males, there is a marked contrast with the general population under the age of 10; in the next decade the females show an excess in the mortality, as the male lives do during the third decennial period.

After the summary of the work of the session, 1860–61, given in the Report of the Council of the Institute of Actuaries, it is stated that Mr. Jellicoe, the president, expressed a strong opinion that Messrs.

*Journal of Statistical Society, 1846, p. 45. The table is compiled from the obituaries of the Annual Register from the date of its first publication in 1758 to the year 1843 inclusive.

Bailey and Day * have proved their case. We must leave it to the judgment of our readers to determine which authority they will accept for their guide in this matter.

Officers of the army present no special feature as regards life insurance, and are only called upon to pay extra rates when they are on duty entailing the contingencies of war, or when they are sent to stations in tropical regions. These rates vary according to the circumstances of the case. Thus, in the Crimean War the rate at first was from 5 to 10 guineas per cent per annum extra, but as the war continued the rate became more severe. During the Abyssinian expedition the addition was 5 guineas extra for not more than a year. During the war of 1866 the German offices appear to have charged an extra rate of 4 guineas; but during the last war between France and Germany 10 guineas was charged for six months for combatant officers, and 10 guineas per annum for medical officers. In India the rate of 2 per cent extra covers death from all causes there.

The officers of H.M. Navy are required to pay the usual rates, with 10s. 6d. per annum within the limits, but a special rate beyond the limits. These limits vary even now at different offices, but there is a general tendency to expand them; but, of course, in case of war, naval officers are mulcted in a higher

* On the Rate of Mortality among the Families of the Peerage, by A. H. Bailey, actuary of the Equity and Law Assurance Societies and Fellow of the Institute of Actuaries; and Archibald Day, Actuary of the London and Law Assurance Society and Fellow of the Institute of Actuaries (Assurance Magazine, July 1871).

rate, like that imposed on officers of the army, to meet the special risk.

Mr. Bailey,* in an article on the rates of extra premium, tells us that in 1741 extra premiums were charged for a voyage to

Flanders and back . .	£1	6	0	per cent.
Ireland and back . .	0	10	0	"
Scarborough by sea . .	0	10	0	"
Gibraltar . . .	2	2	0	"
(And the same as late as 1821.)				
Holland, Germany, and Russia	0	10	0	"

Even now several offices restrict the lives assured to Europe; but, excepting a small extra charge to cover the extra risk of the voyage out and home, most offices include within the limits of the ordinary rate the Azores, Madeira, British North America, and the United States east of the Mississippi and not south of the latitude of Washington, or such parts of South America, the Cape of Good Hope, and Australasia, including New Zealand, as are south of 30 degrees of south latitude.

Thanks to the increasing influence exercised by the medical profession, many of the dangers which formerly beset the military and naval man have been removed or diminished. We have already shown how greatly the expectation of life in the common soldier has been improved within the last twenty years. In Her Majesty's Navy the fell disease scurvy, which formerly more than decimated it, is no longer known, and improved ventilation has done much to increase the wholesomeness of our ships of war. The actual horrors of war, and the consecutive

* Assurance Magazine, vol. xv. p. 78.

effects upon the combatants, have been much diminished by the Red Cross Society and the humane tendencies of the age, though there is little hope of realising the dream of Henry IV. of France and many well-meaning persons of all ages, of establishing universal peace.

In regard to life insurance, it is satisfactory to know that there is here, as elsewhere, an improvement in the prospect of life, and it may be well to take the present occasion of bringing before the reader a little further evidence of the real improvement in sanitary matters, as shown by the influence of modern civilisation upon longevity. A reduction of the rates of insurance has already resulted from the amelioration that has been demonstrated, and it is reasonable to assume that a further reduction,* compatible with safety, and therefore beneficial equally to insurer and insuree will be effected.

Scurvy, dysentery, ague, may in England be re-

* There are two sides to every question; we therefore quote the remarks which Mr. Griffiths Davies makes on this point. "The diminution of mortality has been urged to favour the reduction of the rates for life assurances; but granting that, with the improvement of medical science, and the successful extermination of several diseases by which our predecessors have suffered, connected with increased knowledge and more comfortable means of subsistence, as well as improved habits, greater degree of cleanliness, ventilation, etc., the rate of mortality to have been considerably reduced, it follows that the very fact of its being variable, must strengthen the idea of the *possibility* of its again increasing with other changes of circumstances, which may take place before a considerable proportion of the risk now undertaken by insurance companies shall have been discharged."—(Treatise on Annuities, p. 14.)

garded as enemies of no account, when we consider their former ravages; while syphilis, gout, scrofula, and its congeners, have abated much of their severity under the wiser measures that we now employ to counteract them.

If we look to the history of scurvy, we find that it was formerly very prevalent on shore, owing to the absence of vegetables, and even as late as the 17th century, annually from 50 to 90 deaths took place in London alone from this disease. At sea the mortality resulting from it was frightful; thus in 1726, Admiral Hosier sailed to the West Indies with seven ships, and buried his ship's company twice, when he himself died, worn out by chagrin. In 1741 Lord Anson lost half his crew in six months from scurvy; at the end of the second year of his voyage only 71, out of 961 men who sailed with him, were fit for the least duty. The introduction of lemon juice as a part of a sailor's rations at the beginning of the present century—thanks to Dr. Lind, Sir Gilbert Blane, and others—had so good an effect, that whereas before its use in 1780 there were 1457 cases of scurvy in Haslar Hospital, within eighteen months of its employment there was not one. In connection with this matter, we may again advert to the advantage of good light wine over ardent spirits, which are still too much resorted to in our navy. For when, during the blockade of the River Plate in 1845, by the French and British squadrons, the latter suffered much from scurvy, which the former escaped, owing mainly, as Dr. Bryson has shown, to their daily ration of red wine, while the English sailors had their usual allowance of rum. Sir Gilbert Blane founded a gold medal, to be awarded biennially to medical officers of the navy for meritorious contributions to the literature of their profession; and there has been no worthier recipient of the honour than the medical officer of the Investigator,* Dr., now Sir Alexander Armstrong, who carried his ship's crew through unparalleled hardships, but with unparalleled success, and with comparative immunity from scurvy, under circumstances of great privation, during Captain Maclure's search after the North-west Passage. Unfortunately the merchant service has greatly neglected the rules laid down for the prevention of scurvy, as recent discussions in the journals have demonstrated. So late as 1852 to 1857 inclusive, there were 172 deaths from scurvy in British foreign-going ships, distributed as shown in the following table,† obtained from the log-books and other documents in the office of Captain Hoskins, R.N., Registrar-General of Seamen:—

Years.	Vessels.	Tonnage.	Crews, exclusive of Masters.	Total Deaths.	Deaths from Scurvy.
1852	7580	2,449,364	110,769	2298	17
1853	8357	2,791,224	122,091	3263	10
1854	7418	2,759,120	114,639	2799	35
1855	7957	3,018,951	123,733	3292	50
1856	8551	3,190,011	127,805	3606	32
1857	8100	3,168,105	124,580	3474	28

* Observations on Naval Hygiene and Scurvy. By Alexander Armstrong, M.D., R.N. London, 1858.

† British and Foreign Medical Chirurgical Review, October 1858, p. 397.

Another disease with which, in England, we are now only acquainted in its milder forms, but which formerly was a cause of great mortality in this country, is dysentery or bloody flux. Sydenham,* who lived in the middle of the 17th century, speaks of it as a common disease affecting a large number of people, and the bills of mortality show it to have been one of the most fatal diseases. The annual mortality from 1667-1692 amounted in London to 2000 per annum from this disease.† What the mortality throughout England was, we have as little means of showing as we can give that formerly produced by ague, which Dr. Caius states to have been so fatal in London in the year 1558, that the living could hardly bury the dead. The real nature and cure were so little understood that it even came to be looked upon as rather a beneficial influence, which kept off other diseases, so as to give rise to the adage that

> "An ague in spring
> Is fit for a king."

Without speculating upon this view of the matter, we may remind the reader that James I., and afterwards Cromwell, fell victims to ague. The plague and black death, which are probably synonymous, have been entirely banished from these realms, as well as a dire disease known as the sweating sickness; but without pursuing this important matter further, we limit ourselves to giving a few data ap-

* Medical Observations, chap. 3.

† Heberden on the Increase and Decrease of different Diseases in London. 1801.

plicable to more recent times. The effects of smallpox, which at one time destroyed half our population, have now been reduced to small proportions, though even recent legislation has not put this country—where vaccination was first discovered—on a par with Continental States in which the process has been more thoroughly and carefully carried out.

In the half century from 1750-1800 the deaths from smallpox in England for every 1000 deaths amounted to	96·
From 1800 to 1850 the deaths from smallpox per 1000 were	35·
In the various German States the mortality from smallpox before vaccination was introduced was per 1000 deaths . .	66.5
After vaccination there occurred . .	7.6
In Bohemia and Lombardy vaccination reduced the mortality to	2.0

Vaccination has not only reduced the mortality from smallpox, but also the frequency of smallpox epidemics, for previous to the employment of vaccination, and while inoculation was practised, they occurred at the rate of 84 per 100 years; whereas, since the introduction of vaccination, and since inoculation has been declared illegal, the proportion has sunk to 24 epidemics per 100 years.*

Life insurance offices still suffer loss through this disease, which might by compulsory vaccination, efficiently carried out, be as completely subdued as scurvy has been. It is not creditable to this coun-

* Smallpox and Vaccination; Letter from Dr. Edward Seaton, etc. Parliamentary Paper, 3d May 1853.

try that in 1853 the deaths from smallpox in England still amounted to 3151, but in 1871 the actual number of fatal cases of smallpox reached the alarming number of 23,126.* We do not now attribute such fluctuations to the inscrutable decrees of Providence, since we know that the prevention of these and other epidemics rests with ourselves.

It is satisfactory to turn from this painful subject to the statistics which Mr. Griffith Davies † places before us, showing the gradual and sensible decrease of the mortality and consequent improvement in the expectation of life in this country during the last and a part of the present century. The result of his researches on this point is thus summed up; taking all ages together, out of the same population there died—

From 1720 to 1730	. . . amounting	1068
„ 1730 „ 1740	. . . „	1043
„ 1740 „ 1750	. . . „	924
„ 1750 „ 1760	. . . „	848
„ 1760 „ 1770	. . . „	840
„ 1770 „ 1780	. . . „	857
„ 1780 „ 1790	. . . „	787
„ 1790 „ 1800	. . . „	747
„ 1800 „ 1805	. . . „	697
„ 1805 „ 1810	. . . „	659
„ 1810 „ 1815	. . . „	612
„ 1815 „ 1820	. . . „	623

or a reduction of two-fifths in 100 years, which has gone on increasing since. Thus Dr. Farr ‡ tells us

* Registrar-General's Report, 1871, p. 146.

† Treatise on Annuities, p. 88, by Griffith Davies, F.R.S., London. Published without date.

‡ Twelfth Annual Report of the Registrar-General, 1853.

that at the time when Dr. Price's observations were taken, upon which the Northampton tables were constructed, the average duration of life in Northampton was 30 years, whereas in 1853 it had reached 37½ years.

M. Quetelet's * work affords numerous illustrations of the diminution of mortality in various European communities, which, in part at least, may be attributed to improved hygiene and to greater domestic comfort. The following table, which this author quotes from Moreau de Jonnès, though possibly subject to some correction, will be studied with interest; it shows the changes that have occurred in different countries in the rate of mortality at two distinct periods:—

Name of Country.	Period.	One Death in	Period.	One Death in
Sweden . .	1754 to 1768	34·	1821 to 1825	45·
Denmark .	1751 to 1754	32·	1819	45·
Germany .	1788	32·	1825	45·
Prussia . .	1717	30·	1821 to 1824	39·
Würtemberg .	1749 to 1754	31·	1825	45·
Austria . .	1822	40·	1825 to 1830	43·
Holland .	1800	26·	1824	40·
England .	1690	33·	1821	58·
Great Britain.	1785 to 1789	43·	1800 to 1804	47·
France . .	1776	25·5	1825 to 1827	39·5
Canton deVaud	1756 to 1766	35·	1824	47·
Lombardy .	1767 to 1774	27·5	1827 to 1828	31·
Papal States .	1767	21·5	1829	28·
Scotland .	1801	44·	1821	50·

* Sur l'Homme, vol. i. p. 240.

But much yet remains to be done; for when we find in some parts of England a rate of mortality amounting to 36 per 1000, while there are districts in which it falls as low as 15 per 1000, the difference, which is demonstrably due to preventable causes, is, pro tanto, an indictment against the manner in which our sanitary legislation performs its work, and cannot be regarded otherwise than as a serious imputation upon our much vaunted civilisation.

CHAPTER VI.

THE INSUREE'S LIABILITY TO DISEASE.

It may now be convenient to examine, in order, the various indications of a proclivity to disease in the individual insuree. The most natural arrangement seems to be that suggested by the position of the vital organs, and we will therefore successively consider the head, the thorax, and the abdomen, and append such further remarks on the surface and extremities as the subject appears to require.

Previously to going into detailed consideration of the different items that appear to deserve attention, it may be interesting to the reader to have placed before him a summary of the experience of a number of first-class insurance offices as to the causes which induce claims. It will be seen that although the results present many broad features of resemblance, they differ in too many points to allow us to take their united experience as a standard of comparison. The table is in the main that given by Mr. Smee jun.,* but we have sought to render the numbers more suitable for comparison by adding a calculation of their percentage proportion, for which we are indebted to the kind assistance of Mr. Fennell, and the

*Report of Gresham Life Assurance Society, by A. H. Smee jun., F.C.S. London, 1868.

COMPARATIVE TABLE OF DEATHS OF VARIOUS COMPANIES.

Partially extracted by A. H. Smee, jun., F.C.S., in report of Gresham Life Assurance Society. London, 1868.

	Gresham.		Scottish Amicable.		Scottish Equitable.		Clerk's Insured. Various Sources.		Equitable.		Gotha.		Scottish Widows' Fund.		Briton.	
	No.	Per Cent.	No.	Per Cent.	No.	Per Cent.	No.	Per Cent.	No.	Per Cent.	No.	Per Cent.	No.	Per Cent.	No.	Per Cent.
Zymotic . .	121	12·1	157	20·31	245	13.21	137	13·59	499	12·18	521	21·08	163	11·66	138	11·84
Uncertain seat .	67	6·7	34	4·39	125	6·74	62	6·15	456	11·13	380	15·38	82	5·86	58	4·98
Tubercular .	158	15·8	107	13·84	219	11·32	257	25·5	339	8·28	437	17·69	96	6·87	226	19·39
Nervous system .	198	19·8	130	16·82	390	21·02	147	14·58	821	20·05	375	15·17	303	21·67	169	14·51
Circulatory system	62	6·2	67	8·66	220	11·86	63	6·25	149	3·64	69	2·79	221	15·81	98	8·41
Respiratory system	200	20·	78	10·09	219	11·81	125	12·4	508	12·4	251	10·16	180	12·87	168	14·42
Digestive system	83	8·3	97	12·55	220	11·86	87	8·63	407	9·94	207	8·38	172	12·3	113	9·69
Urinary system .	43	4·3	23	2·97	99	5·34	41	4·07	148	3·61	30	1·61	87	6·2	40	3·43
Generative system	5	·5	3	·39	8	·43	2	·19	4	·09	10	·41	2	·14	15	1·28
Age, sudden death, etc. . .	19	1·9	16	2·07	44	2·37	27	2·68	609	14·87	86	3·48	49	3·51	72	6·16
Violence . .	38	3·8	43	5.56	70	3·77	54	5·36	76	1·88	87	3·52	40	2·86	61	5·24
Unknown causes	6	·6	18	2.33	5	·27	6	·59	79	1·93	8	·32	3	·21	7	·72
Totals . .	1000		773		1855		1008		4095		2471		1398		1165	

experience of the Briton Life Office, with which we have been favoured by Mr. John Messent.

The cerebral diseases of childhood that chiefly affect the future man, even though they have remained in abeyance for a long time, are of a convulsive character. Convulsions and fits are epileptiform diseases which frequently produce in early life the subsequent development of true epilepsy. Our client may have suffered from the former, owing to stomach derangement, worms, teething, or other eccentric irritation, and never afterwards have manifested the slightest tendency to anything of the kind, in which case our estimate of his longevity need not on that account be affected. But if he subsequently, at or before puberty, has shown the slightest trace of temporary obliviousness or loss of consciousness, the suspicion of an epileptic tendency is aroused. And whenever we have the certainty of a single epileptic seizure, the life, spite of the modern advances in the treatment of this disease, must be considered a damaged one. If the attacks occur at very long intervals, or appear to have been checked altogether, the life must still be taken at a high rate, because we have no certainty that it may not return at any period of life, and directly or indirectly abridge life. A confirmed epileptic, however good his general health, is altogether uninsurable; not because he will necessarily die of his disease, but because it exposes him to danger by fire and water, by the road and in his house, from which it is impossible to guard him.

There are no satisfactory facts by which we can determine a tendency to brain disease in a comparatively healthy young person, apart from his personal or hereditary history. It is generally considered,* and our experience to some extent accords with the popular view, that a certain habit of body, a short neck, and a plethoric appearance, indicates an apoplectic tendency. But we should not think it just to refuse such an individual on that plea alone. If he exhibited any symptoms of what is called determination of blood to the head, vertiginous attacks, headache, throbbing in the head, and the like, our opinion as to his expectation of life would be modified, and if he gave the slightest reason for our suspecting a fondness of liquor, we should advise his rejection. During manhood, when the question of temperance plays so important a part, indications of previous delirium tremens and of present alcoholism, may be found in the breath, the furred tongue, the dyspepsia, the tremor, the unsteady handwriting, and the general mode of expression and habitus of the candidate.

Infantile paralysis is a condition that may entirely have yielded to treatment; but any symptoms of paralysis, whether depending upon an abnormal con-

* Dr. Fleming (Medical Statistics of Life Insurance, p. 47) remarks on this point, "The commonly received opinion that persons of peculiar physical conformation—those with short necks, full and corpulent habit of body, large head and ruddy countenances—are prone to apoplexy and other head diseases, is no doubt correct; but the converse by no means holds so true, as is generally believed, for we find many individuals are the subjects of these affections of the head, who are free from the above physical characteristics—in fact the tall, thin, and athletic are, in my observation, about as often attacked as the plethoric."

dition of the brain or spinal cord that are manifested subsequently, should be a bar to insurance; or if, under certain favourable circumstances, admissible at all, can only be taken at very advanced rates.

The danger from disease of the brain increases with age, and is specially associated with degenerative conditions that manifest themselves in the arterial system. All indications of premature decay must be carefully watched; and if associated with any special symptoms pointing to irregular performance of the cerebral functions, they must be held as diminishing the prospect of longevity.

As with all organs, the healthy employment of the brain does not tend to impair its vigour. Professional men and philosophers, who perform much brain work, are generally long lived. But when associated with harassing anxieties, the nutrition gives way, and sometimes apoplexy and paralysis set in. Where the emotions come into play largely, as in the artist and poet, brain power appears to yield more readily to the tax imposed upon it than in other professions, for they are not as a body a long-lived race.

About one-eighth of the total mortality is due to diseases of the nervous system. In 1871* the deaths from all causes amounted to 517,879, of which 62,443 were due to this class of affections, distributed as follows:—

* Registrar-General's Report for 1871, p. 146.

	Males.	Females.	Total.
Cephalitis . .	2,637	2,177	4,814
Apoplexy . .	5,610	5,879	11,489
Paralysis . .	5,854	5,869	11,723
Insanity . .	443	523	966
Chorea . .	22	60	82
Epilepsy . .	1,338	1,120	2,458
Convulsions . .	14,251	11,058	25,309
Unclassified brain disease	3,279	2,323	5,602
		Total, .	62,443

It is scarcely necessary to point out that the occurrence of a single apoplectic or paralytic seizure, even if a good recovery has taken place, ought to render such a life uninsurable, on account of the great probability of a succeeding attack, which is likely to prove fatal.

Connected with this subject we must allude to sunstroke, a somewhat anomalous condition, pathologically speaking, which occurs in our own country, but more frequently among our soldiers and other countrymen serving in tropical or sub-tropical regions. The individual thus attacked may make a complete recovery, but the affection is very liable to leave behind it impaired brain power, if not actual paralytic or epileptiform conditions, which materially affect longevity. Its influence on life insurance must be estimated according to the traces that remain after sufficient time has elapsed for a cure of the primary affection.

Dr. Fleming presents us with the following table,

showing the absolute and relative number of deaths from diseases of the brain and nervous system occurring in all England and two large life offices, from which it follows that the mortality among the assured, due to this cause, is disproportionately large. Such evidence ought to act as a special stimulus to the medical advisers of insurance offices to search out the early indications of cerebral mischief.

Ages.	Number of Deaths from Diseases of Brain, etc.			Percentage of Deaths from Diseases of the Brain, etc.		
	England. Average of seven years, 1848 to 1854.	Gotha Society.	Scottish Amicable.	England.	Gotha Society.	Scottish Amicable.
15 to 25	1,469	0	0	5·09	0·00	0·00
25 to 35	1,709	11	13	5·92	7·33	11·60
35 to 45	2,224	51	32	8·20	10·30	15·38
45 to 55	2,797	103	26	10·54	15·91	14·60
55 to 65	3,978	125	27	13.14	17·40	19·56
65 to 75	5,257	85	32	14·48	18·20	26·66
Total.	17,434	375	130	9·80	15·20	16·81

In the case of brain disease, as of other morbid conditions, an early manifestation of the scrofulous taint would diminish our estimate of the individual's liability; and therefore, although in the majority of instances all traces of scrofula have disappeared at the time the individual becomes a candidate for insurance, the fact of his having suffered from some lymphatic disorder in early life must not be overlooked. Persistent enlargement of the external glands, of the tonsils, scrofulous ulceration, and caries in childhood, are so many indications of impaired nutrition, and not unfrequently give a key to later derangements and their probable influence upon the duration of life.

All bona fide disease of the spinal cord must be regarded as an absolute bar to insurance, on account of its generally incurable character, and its tendency to death. Much, however, is called spinal disease, especially in women, which ought to be included rather in the categories of hysteria and anæmia than in the class of diseases dependent upon structural changes in the spinal marrow. It does not belong to our province to do more than draw attention to the necessity of carefully discriminating between the genuine and imitative affection. The tendency, on the part of the insuree, would be rather in the direction of trying to make light of what the well-trained practitioner would regard as a more serious symptom. He must therefore be on his guard not to pass lightly over doubtful points bearing upon this question. This applies particularly to the early symptoms of tabes dorsalis, or, as it is now called, locomotor ataxy, the early symptoms of which may easily be misinterpreted. If there is the least sign of a want of co-ordinating power accompanying vague, so-called rheumatic pains, the case should be unconditionally rejected; or if the adviser chooses to give the candidate the benefit of his doubt, the latter may be required to present himself for further examination in six months' time, when the symptoms will have declared themselves sufficiently to allow of an absolute and final decision.

According to the Registrar-General's Report of 1871, Thoracic Disease carried off 161,480 persons, or nearly one-third of the total mortality; of these 26,219 suffered from disease of the heart and great vessels; 53,376 succumbed to phthisis, or pulmonary consumption; and 81,825 to other pulmonary affections. It is not, therefore, surprising that all life insurance companies pay especial attention to the condition of the thoracic viscera, and that their medical officers are expected to seek out every indication that the family history, and the antecedents and present condition, of a candidate may afford on this point. These possess the further melancholy advantage of being particularly trustworthy, as modern science has done more to facilitate the diagnosis of diseases of the chest than that of the viscera of the other cavities of the body.

We will consider them in their relation to life insurance in the order just mentioned.

1. Diseases of the heart and great vessels.—To this class about one-sixth of the total mortality is due, a proportion that is much larger than appears to prevail in insurance offices, if we may trust our own experience, supported as it is by the Analysis of Deaths in the Scottish Widows' Fund.* According to Dr. Begbie, the total deaths among 5989 persons insured amounted in 30 years to 642, of which 53, or about the twelfth part, or 8·25 per cent, were attributed to lesions of the heart and

*Observations on the Mortality of the Scottish Widows' Fund, by James Begbie, M.D. Monthly Journal of Medical Science, January 1847.

vessels.* The large majority of heart diseases in this country are due to the rheumatic poison, which, in the form of rheumatic fever or acute rheumatic arthritis, is chiefly prevalent during the second and third decennium of life; and though it often passes off without physical evidence at the time of inflammation of the heart or its membranes, rarely leaves them altogether unscathed. Cases are common in which, when no peri- or endo- carditis has been detected during the fever, cardiac lesions can be traced later in life to the former occurrence of rheumatic fever. Moreover, the rheumatic poison is apt to cause a recurrence of the disease in the same individual, and no immunity is afforded by an attack, as is the case in some febrile disorders. The report of rheumatic fever having occurred in a candidate is therefore always to be regarded with consideration, and should direct special attention to the heart. A single well-marked attack, in which the patient has been confined to bed for six weeks or more, justifies an addition of about seven years; if the attack has recurred, and especially if an hereditary tendency to rheumatism also exists, a higher rate is proper, even if the heart shows no indication of valve lesion. Co-existent defect in the valves, as demonstrated by the ear and other physical signs easily recognised by the physician, justify the rejection of the life, or its

* Dr. Fleming (Medical Statistics of Life Assurance, p. 52) finds the percentage of deaths from this cause, compared with deaths from all causes, to be, for all England, from 1848 to 1854, 5·60; for the Gotha Society, 2·79; and for the Scottish Amicable, 8·40.

acceptance only at what most persons would consider prohibitory rates.

All forms of valvular disease may, on the one hand, prove the main instruments in causing a rapid death, or, on the other, as is well known to every physician engaged in extensive practice, remain for an indefinite period subjectively latent. Of all valve lesions, aortic regurgitation is the one to which sudden death is most frequently due. "I have known death," observes Dr. Walshe, in drawing attention to this fact,* "take place during the act of walking, of eating, of speaking; while the patient was emotionally excited, and, per contra, at a moment when he was perfectly calm. And a very singular proposition is, that the more pure and uncomplicated the regurgitation, the freer the heart from any other form of disease, the more likely is the individual to be cut off without a moment's warning." We may add, in the words of the same author, an important practical fact, which the unpracticed ausculator is apt to lose sight of, that there is "no direct connection between the amount of danger of disease at an orifice of the heart and the intensity of an existing murmur; the very weakness of a murmur may, indeed, be a fatal sign."

All well-marked symptoms of cardiac disease, whether attributable to rheumatism, to gout, to alcoholism, or other causes, a fortiori, if shown to be complicated with disturbance of the liver, the brain, of kidneys, render a life inadmissible. Where a doubt exists, in the interpretation of certain signs,

* On Diseases of the Heart, 3d edition, p. 389, and *seqq.*

the case may be deferred, or a consideration of the patient's habits and occupation may assist in establishing a reasonably safe conclusion. A single examination may not suffice to determine whether a murmur is due to anæmia or to organic lesion. If the former, it will be removed by proper treatment; but the exigencies of the case must be met by postponement of acceptance of the policy until the murmur has disappeared. One of the forms of degenerative disease, which frequently leads to a fatal issue, fatty degeneration of the heart tissue, does not always offer physical signs of a marked character. It is essentially a disease of advanced life due to a retrograde metamorphosis of the tissues. A premature arcus senilis, though not a safe guide, is sometimes found associated with cardiac softening, and at any rate manifests early senility, which may diminish the applicant's chances of life. All indications of a feeble and irregular circulation, as shown by occasional syncope, excited and easily excitable pulse, palpitation, pulsatile feelings in different parts of the body, are of more or less importance, proportionate to their severity and frequency. It is common to attribute symptoms of this kind to "nervousness," and therefore of no importance; but "nervousness" is in itself a sign of constitutional debility, which, unless traceable to a temporary and accidental influence, as we have known it in a perfectly healthy person to arise from coffee, militates against the soundness of the life; and experience tells us that a persistently high pulse, even when not apparently connected with any organic disease, is often the forerunner of serious mischief either in the heart or lungs. A pulse that habitually is at or above 90, is unhealthy; and if, in the adult man, the normal pulse of 70, under the examination for insurance runs up to 90 and more, it shows an emotional impressibility which argues against his powers of resisting the inroads of disease. The more impressionable character of woman would diminish the importance of this test, though there, too, it must not be taken as a matter of course. The intermittent pulse, again, is one that deserves careful consideration; it may be accidental, from the use of certain nervine agents, as green tea or tobacco, or only result from the temporary effect of an attack of dyspepsia; but, although there are cases on record of persons having enjoyed good health with an intermittent pulse throughout their life, it is generally associated with imperfect nutrition and innervation of the heart, and a sign or forerunner of fatty degeneration of the organ, angina, ossification of the arteries and analogous conditions, which yield little information to the stethoscope, though frequently the cause of much suffering and death.

We should be inclined to regard the irregular and remittent pulse as even more significant of malnutrition of the heart and imperfect circulation than the varieties previously spoken of, and even without other marked evidence of disease sufficient to justify rejection. A similar conclusion must, of course, be arrived at where a closer examination of the heart itself reveals aortic or mitral insufficiency, or where percussion and auscultation indicate the presence of hypertrophy or dilatation.

If the medical officer have a doubt as to the state of the circulation, and rest does not restore the balance, the effect of brisk exercise, as running up and down stairs, will generally bring out the irregularities more prominently, and determine their nature. A simply nervous pulse may lose its irritable character when action takes the place of emotion, but an abnormal pulse that depends upon organic mischief will exhibit its peculiarities in a more marked degree when a greater demand is made upon the circulation.

Excessive slowness of the pulse, *i.e.*, a pulse below 60, is rarely met with unassociated with serious disease. Where it occurs, the medical man must exercise his own judgment in the interpretation of the symptoms, as it is too infrequent to enable us to lay down any specific indications. In the absence of any other traceable sign of disease it need not affect the expectation of life, and may be set down to idiosyncrasy of the insuree.

It is to be borne in mind by the young practitioner, that irregular distribution of the arteries are by no means infrequent. The radial artery may dip down so deeply, or be so small as not to be felt; though the irregular distribution is generally symmetrical, we often find it in one arm and not in the other. If one artery cannot be felt, we must look for another, and with a little care the mystery is easily solved. Cases in which the pulse is absent, from plugging of the arteries, are not likely to be met with in the examination-room of an insurance company.

Dyspnœa is a symptom that may depend upon imperfect performance of the cardiac or pulmonary functions. In either case, if not accounted for by preceding violent exercise, it shows actual disease of the heart or lungs, or a disturbance in the balance of the circulation and respiration, which depends upon disorder of other organs capable of influencing the circulation; thus we have breathlessness of cardiac, of pulmonary, of hepatic, of cerebral, and of hæmic origin. Its source and nature must be determined according to those rules of diagnosis which are taught in systematic works on medicine, and by the bedside. Where it is due to temporary influences, brief rest will speedily remove it, and equable respiration and a calm pulse take the place of the previous turmoil.

2. Phthisis.—We have already noted that 53,376 persons died of pulmonary consumption in 1871 out of a total mortality of 517,819, which is close upon two-sixths of the mortality from thoracic disease, or one-ninth of the mortality from all causes in England and Wales. No single disease claims so many victims, but it is consolatory to find that it does not appear to be on the increase; for, in 1853,* when the deaths from all causes amounted only to 421,097, the mortality from phthisis was 54,918, or less than the eighth part; of these, 25,955 were males, and 28,963 females; the relative numbers of the sexes in 1871 being 26,668 males, and 26,708 females.

* Registrar-General's Sixteenth Annual Report, p. 124.

As phthisis is not liable to epidemic fluctuations, we may indulge in a hope that this amelioration is due to a real improvement in the sanitary and social condition of our population. In life assurance the claims result large from phthisis, and it is here that medical selection tells more according to the manner in which it is conducted than in any other form of disease; a point that is well brought out by Dr. Begbie,* by a comparison of two analyses of the claims occurring at different periods in the history of the Scottish Widows' Fund; and also by Dr. Christison's Analysis of the deaths in the Standard.† The proportions of the sexes are necessarily inverted, as the male lives predominate so largely over the female insurees. Thus in the Scottish Widows' fund,‡ out of 72 deaths from consumption, 61 were males and 11 females. In regard to age, the statistics of Dr. Begbie accord with those of the Registrar-General, who shows that the largest proportion of deaths occurs between 30 and 40. The highest mortality, according to the experience of the Equitable, takes place between the ages 40 and 50.

The following table, extracted from Dr. Chambers' Decennium Pathologicum,§ gives further proof that youth is not to be regarded as the "harvest time" of consumption, and that the proportionate mortality from that disease does not vary between the ages of 15 and 70 as much as is generally assumed:

* Edinburgh Monthly Journal, Aug. 1853. † *Ibid.*

‡ Observations, etc., by J. Begbie, M.D.

§ Medical Times, Aug. 14, 1872; and Dr. Fuller's work on Diseases of the Chest, p. 350.

Age.	Number of Patients Examined.			Tuberculosis in the Lungs.				Percentage of Pulmonary Tuberculosis.		
	Males.	Females.	Total.	Males.	Females.	Sex unknown.	Total.	Males.	Females.	Total.
Birth to 15	94	60	154	20	17	0	37	21·2	28·3	24·0
15 to 30	377	259	636	128	82	1	211	33·9	31·5	33·1
30 to 45	472	179	651	120	35	0	155	25·4	19·5	23·8
45 to 65	299	139	438	66	11	0	77	22·0	7·9	17·5
above 60	109	58	167	10	1	0	11	9·1	1·7	6·5
Age unknown	74	37	111	14	10	2	26	18·9	27·0	23·4
Total	1425	732	2157	358	156	3	517	25·1	21·3	23·9

In the chapter devoted to the consideration of hereditary transmission, we have dwelt upon the special tendency to hereditariness in phthisis. It is here, therefore, peculiarly necessary that the family as well as the personal antecedents of the future policyholder should be carefully investigated. And we would warn the medical officer against yielding to the popular impression that this inquiry becomes unnecessary after full manhood is reached, as the danger of phthisis continues beyond the age of 60; an impression that weighs much with boards of directors, who will admit evidence of a consumptive taint from puberty to 25, which they frequently put aside as insignificant after that period.

In a person in the slightest degree predisposed, any debilitating influence, especially if it interferes with the due oxygenation of the blood and induces pulmonary congestion, is likely to give rise to phthisis. Scrofula in early life, protracted dyspepsia, repeated catarrhs, imperfect convalescence from continued and exanthematic fevers, indoor occupation of all kinds, especially if carried on in a cramped posture and in a close heated atmosphere, an occupation entailing the inhalation of dust, grit, or metallic particles, are among the numerous causes that lead up to confirmed consumption in one or other of its varieties. Anxiety, supervening upon any of these influences, imperfect food, intemperance, though not in themselves adequate to give rise to the deposit of tubercle, add much to the power of the previously-mentioned *incitamenta mali*. In the female, catamenial derangement and gastric ulceration are to be specially regarded as forerunners of this malady.

The evidences we look for in the individual, as suggesting a suspicion of a phthisical tendency, are, slight morning cough, often disregarded by himself; frequent hoarseness; general want of vigour without apparent reason; loss of flesh; an habitually quick pulse; the occurrence of hæmoptysis; breathlessness on slight exertion, or still more, an habitual acceleration of respiration. The more of these symptoms that are associated in the same person, the greater the probability of the approach of phthisis, if its actual presence be not already capable of detection by auscultation and percussion. The frequent recurrence of sore throats is a point deserving of attention; if dependent upon chronic enlargement of the tonsils, it is a sign of scrofulous taint; if more associated with irritation and inflammation of the larynx and trachea, it shows a delicacy and susceptibility of the mucous membrane of the part, which commonly depends upon the same constitutional influences that may lead to phthisis.

A phthisical habit is often recognisable by the transparency of the sclerotic and languid expression of the large eye, the liquid eye of the poet; by the clear complexion, with bright patchy redness, or the opposite condition of a pale muddy hue; the easily dilated nostril; the general prominence of all the bones, owing to the adipose tissue disappearing; the long, thin neck; the *je ne sais quoi* of general fragility. But it is dangerous to rely too much on such indications; for although in the majority of instances the experienced practitioner will not err far in his diagnosis of a case by a mere general survey, the error in the case before us involves so many important interests that he is bound to ascertain any further evidence that may be at hand. Every practitioner will be able to bring to mind instances in which first cursory impressions proved to be fallacious. Among the indications, we would single out three—the habitually quick pulse, the loss of flesh, and the occurrence of hæmoptysis, as meriting a few further observations.

The healthy adult exhibits a pulse ranging about 70; physical or emotional excitement may raise it temporarily, but if permanently at or above 80 it becomes suspicious, as indicating constitutional debility; and if associated with respirations that exceed the normal frequency of from 15 to 20 per minute, the presumption of the existence of pulmonary incapacity becomes still stronger. A pulse of 100 and upwards ought to militate against the acceptance of any life, unless rest and repeated examinations demonstrate its accidental character. The fulness, the compressibility, and the strength of the pulse must be regarded, as well as the frequency. The pulse of phthisis is weak, easily compressible, and deficient in volume, as well as frequent. In a person with full, hard, round pulse, however frequent, we should scarcely expect to find the auscultatory signs of incipient tubercular mischief. Loss of weight is a very constant sign of the premonitory, or, as it has also been termed, the pre-tubercular stage of phthisis. A healthy adult who enjoys an adequate quantity of wholesome food, and takes a proper amount of exercise, remains stationary in bulk, or increases; a sudden loss of a few pounds even, not accounted for by a change in the habits of life, or great bodily fatigue, shows that some abnormal influence is at work which materially interferes with nutrition. A weight that is much below the average at and after 30, especially if accompanied by an accelerated pulse and breathing, undoubtedly justifies an increased rate, even if no other signs of a tainted constitution are found. Our experience of the policies that have become claims have forced the conviction upon us, that medical men and insurance offices would do well to regard these points more seriously than is generally done in estimating the expectation of life. We have before us an analysis of the 1165 deaths that occurred in the Briton * Life Company from 1863 to 1867 inclusive, and find a mortality due to phthisis alone of 218, or 18·8 per cent. No argument could impress the necessity of paying strict attention to every and the earliest indication of phthisical taint than such numbers.

Hæmoptysis is one of those symptoms of lung disease which the general public naturally regards with much apprehension. If the blood comes up with a slight cough or apparently without an effort, if it is of bright colour, if it is more or less frothy from the admixture of air, the probability is greatly in favour of the assumption that it proceeds from the lungs, whether the quantity be large or small. Whether the hæmoptysis precede the deposit of tubercle or

*Bonus Report for 1867.

accompanies it is a matter of consequence in the treatment and prognosis of the patient's condition, but of little importance in the expectation of the life of the individual, because he ought, unless in very exceptional cases, to be regarded as uninsurable. Applicants often try to slur over the inquiry into the occurrence of hæmoptysis, or they explain it by referring it to epistaxis, to hæmorrhage from a tooth or from the gums, or to sore throat; and from the common difficulty of tracing positive tubercular mischief at the time of its occurrence, or finding the fine crepitus which occasionally enables us to fix the exact spot in the lungs from whence it is derived, they are not unfrequently countenanced in their delusion by their medical attendant. Unless there is positive evidence either that the hæmoptysis was not hæmoptysis at all, but hæmatemesis, or that it really did proceed from the nasi-oral or faucial cavities, it is safe to act upon the assumption that "spitting of blood" was attributable to pulmonary mischief, and a forerunner or accompaniment of tubercular deposit. "There cannot be a doubt," says Dr. Fuller,* "that in the majority of cases in which spitting of blood occurs, however small the quantity may be, tubercles, in an active or latent state, are present in the lungs." It is unnecessary to multiply quotations from high authorities on this question; they would all point in the same direction, in accordance with the daily experience of physicians in active practice.

Although the physical examination of the appli-

*Diseases of the Chest, p. 259.

cant often fails to yield positive evidence of the presence of tubercle in the early stage of phthisis, the chest should always be bared in all cases of life insurance, in order that the configuration of the thoracic walls, the rate and mode of breathing, the condition of the surface as to complexion, venosity, and plumpness, may be accurately determined, as well as the evidence obtainable by percussion and auscultation.

The features that would be suspicious of a phthisical tendency are a general flattening of the chest walls, and especially at the upper front, with diminished expansion during inspiration; a hollow supra- and infra-clavicular space; a bulbous condition of the sternal ends of the ribs; diminished capacity of the chest, as indicated by external measurement and by the spirometer.* There may be some doubt as to how far the spirometer may be used as an index of future consumption; but there appears to be no doubt that "a vital capacity" below the average indicates a generally feeble constitution, less capable of resisting deteriorating influences to which the individual may be exposed, as is well shown in Dr. Balfour's † contribution to the study of spiro-

* Dr. Brinton (Medical Selection of Lives, etc.) lays greater stress on the employment of the spirometer in life insurance examinations than we should be disposed to do. None would deny its value if properly used; but as it requires a certain training, not only on the part of the medical man, but still more on the part of the examinee, to insure its indications being true, it is very apt to yield false results where time is an object to be considered.

† Medico-Chirurgical Transactions, 1860, p. 263.

metry. A number of recruits (amounting to 1126) were tested by the spirometer, and their subsequent medical history, extending on an average to three years and five months, carefully watched. The men were divided into three classes—1. Those whose vital capacity was more than 10 inches under the average calculated for men of the same height by Mr. Hutchinson's tables; 2. Those whose capacity ranged between 10 cubic inches under, and 10 above the average; 3. Those whose "vital capacity" exceeded the average by more than 10 inches. The number that died in each class of consumption while in the army was nearly the same, but a much larger proportion of the first class were invalided for this cause,—the invaliding having been four times as high among men under the average as among the others, as shown in the following table:—*

	Aggregate strength.	By consumption.			Ratio per 1000 of strength.		
		Died.	Invalided.	Total.	Died.	Invalided.	Total.
Below the average	1511	19	17	26	12·57	11·25	23·82
Average	1145	14	3	17	12·23	1·62	14·85
Above the average	1206	17	3	20	14·09	2·49	16·58

* As this table may not be at once clear to some of my readers unfamiliar with statistical inquiries, I add the following explanation, with which my friend Dr. Balfour has kindly favoured me:—"The number of men in each class were under observation for different periods of time; it is therefore necessary to reduce them to unity to show the annual ratio of deaths. This could be done either by multiplying the strength, *i.e.*, the numbers over whom the observations extended, by the numbers of years and fractions of years during which they

The average circumference of the chest above the nipples is 38 inches, but considerable variations are possible without by themselves indicating disease. The signs of quiescent tubercular deposit elicited by percussion are a want of resiliency in the chest walls in the infra-clavicular regions, a greater or less absence of the normal resonance, at the same spot, or in the supra-scapular spaces, which is specially sig-

were under observation, or by dividing the total number of deaths in each class by the same number, and thus obtaining the number of deaths in each year. I have preferred the former plan, as I object to talking of the death of a fractional part of a man. We talk of this constantly in the ratio of deaths per 1000 of strength, but this is merely a proportional statement, whereas the other is supposed to be an actual statement of the deaths. In case this is not quite clear, I would put it thus:—The number of men over whom my observations extended was in

1st class . .	416	1126
2d " . .	342	
3d " . .	368	

but the deaths in these classes occurred in different periods of time—

In the 416 in 3·632 years.
" 342 in 3·348 "
" 368 in 3·277 "

The first would be equal to 1511 men under observation for one year, the second to 1145, and the third to 1206 for the same period. Or it may be stated thus:—The deaths in *each* complete year under observation were in the

1st class . .	8·5352
2d " . .	6·8699
3d " . .	7·3238

I think the multiplication of the strength, or numbers under observation, looks better than the division of the deaths by the period of observation."

nificative when it is unsymmetrical, as it then can scarcely be due, unless there is ricketty malformation, to anything but consolidation of the subjacent pulmonary tissues.* The stethoscope exhibits more or less defective respiratory murmur, or it may be exaggerated at one side while it is feeble on the other; interrupted or jerking respiration, as if the process were effected by instalments, is an early sign of tubercular deposit; and an unduly prolonged expiratory murmur also justifies a suspicion of consolidation; if with these symptoms we find rales of various kinds, moist or dry, the diagnosis of serious mischief is confirmed, but the coincidence of two or more of the deviations from the normal standard

* Dr. Allen* gives the following table of measurements of the chest at different heights and the corresponding weights, which are slightly below those we have given for æt. 30:—

Height.	Weight.	Circumference of Chest.
5 feet 1 inch	120 lbs.	34·06
5 „ 2 inches	125 „	35·13
5 „ 3 „	130 „	35·70
5 „ 4 „	135 „	36·26
5 „ 5 „	140 „	36·83
5 „ 6 „	143 „	37·50
5 „ 7 „	145 „	38·16
5 „ 8 „	148 „	38·53
5 „ 9 „	155 „	39·10
5 „ 10 „	160 „	39·66
5 „ 11 „	165 „	40·23
6 „ „	170 „	40·80

* Medical Examination for Life Insurance. New York, 1872, p. 67.

that have been alluded to ought to entail abso_ute rejection. The character of the voice passing through the stethoscope must also be taken into account; whether the vocal resonance be exaggerated or diminished, it equally shows an abnormal condition, which, occurring at the apices of the lungs, must generally be regarded as indicating tubercle, though, of course, there are other anomalies to which the symptom may be attributable. The medical man in all cases must exercise his judgment, and not allow himself to be determined by a single symptom, unless it be of a very precise character, or more definite than it usually is in the class of individuals which we are reviewing. In all cases, in using the stethoscope as well as in employing percussion, it is necessary for the medical man to compare both sides of the front as well as the back of the chest, and be guided by the differences rather than the actual character of the physical signs.

Candidates for insurance are not likely to present themselves while actually suffering from any acute chest diseases; if they do so the medical officer would necessarily postpone the consideration of the case until recovery had taken place. In the lower parts of the chest recent pneumonia and former pleurisy may leave traces, which need not necessarily affect the expectation. In every chest affection the possibility of a co-existing consumptive taint increases any existing risk manifold, and thus the remains of old pleurisy, in checking the movements of the chest walls, may assist in developing a morbid tendency. In themselves pleuritic adhesions, which even induce a certain amount of dulness and flattening of the lower chest walls, are of no consequence. Few people pass through life without some pleuritic mischief; the history and antecedents of the examinee must be taken into account in determining the exact bearing of individual deviations from the normal standard.

CHAPTER VII.

THE INSUREE'S LIABILITY TO DISEASE—(*Continued*).

THE organs of digestion do not take a high rank in the army of diseases against which the medical adviser of an insurance company has to be on his guard. According to the table given at page 117, the claims resulting from diseases of the digestive system yield precedence in point of fatality to zymotic disease, tubercular affections, diseases of the nervous and of the respiratory systems, with the notable exceptions presented by the Scottish offices, one of which gives a percentage of 12·5 of claims from diseases of the digestive system as against 10·1 per cent in the respiratory system, while another exhibits a percentage of 11·8 of the former to a percentage of 11·3 of claims from tubercular disease ;* the third

* Upon this point the following remarks of Dr. Fleming (Medical Statistics of Life Assurance, p. 59) may throw some light. He finds, by his analysis, that there is a considerable mortality from diseases of the digestive organs "in the Gotha and Scottish Amicable over that of the general population; and when estimated by the deaths from all causes the whole assurance societies show an excess, the Gotha and London Equitable the smallest." This Dr. Fleming considers to be accounted for " by dropsy being entered by the Registrar-General in Class II., and by the two societies last named as a

shows very nearly the same percentage as the digestive over the respiratory, while it considerably exceeds the tubercular class. According to the Registrar-General's analysis of the reports* of the fourteen years ending in 1871, diseases of the digestive organs occupy uniformly the fifth place in the order of fatality of the classes mentioned. And yet their importance must not be measured only by the number of deaths directly referable to them, for if dyspepsia and disease of the liver be not the immediate cause of death, they are, even in those diseases to which death is attributed, but too often the forerunner or the predisposing cause. Rheumatism and gout for instance, with their various sequelæ affecting vital organs, alcoholism and its influence on kidneys, heart, and brain, are a few of the diseases which, though passing under other names, might reasonably be set down among the category under consideration. Dyspepsia must not, therefore, be lightly treated by the insurance officer, and unless palpably due to a solitary error in diet, should be estimated by the rules laid down in its bearing on longevity. It is not our province to enter into the question of the diagnosis

distinct disease, while by the Scottish offices it is correctly referred to the diseases of the organs on which it depended." Still he finds the mortality among the assured from diseases of the digestive organs to be considerably in excess of that of the general population. "Excluding dropsy, 1144 out of 12,243, being 9.34 per cent, died of these diseases against 7·32 in the population of England. Including a third of the cases of dropsy, the deaths numbered 1374 out of 12,243, being 11·22 against 8·77."

* Report for 1871, p. 240.

of the different forms of stomach disease, but wherever there is any trace, such as indicated in systematic works on medicine, of organic disease of the viscus, rejection of the life must follow.

If there is any history of hæmatemesis the symptoms should be carefully analysed, and though it is not of the same importance as hæmoptysis, still it will always render a life doubtful, and under the most favourable circumstances justify an addition. It is usually indicative of ulceration of the stomach, which may have yielded completely, and resulted in a perfect cure, as we frequently see in anæmic young women. All simple ulcers of the stomach will, under appropriate treatment, heal, and their cicatrices are a matter of common observation in post mortems of persons dying of other affections, so that unless the digestion is permanently impaired, and there is evidence of other lesions, they need not call for rejection. Ulcer of the stomach* is stated by Dr. Brinton, on the authority of an extensive analysis of the published experience of various writers, to occur in the proportion of about five per cent in all deaths, of which one-half, approximatively, are to be found in the form of healed scars. It occurs twice as frequently in the female as in the male sex; and spirit drinking and destitution appear to be its chief causes; the maximum frequency occurring in the spirit drinking population of Copenhagen; while its larger proportion in German hospitals appears due to the greater age and more destitute circumstances of their inmates,

* Brinton, on Ulcer of the Stomach, p. 7. London, 1857.

than exhibited by the persons usually received into English hospitals.

In candidates for insurance we have especially to look for the minor indications of gastric derangement. The furred tongue, a glazy irritable surface, an aphthous condition of the tongue and buccal mucous membrane, recurrent inflammation of the fauces, foul breath, especially if tainted with the alcoholic odour, an habitually bitter or acrid taste, waterbrash, acid eructations, flatulent distention, are among the symptoms which deserve attention, and should at least temporarily disqualify for life insurance, until the applicant is able to show a clean bill of health. A fortiori, any evidence of more serious mischief would prove a disqualification, and this view would be strengthened if the habits, the mode of life, and the occupation, are such as to favour the development of dyspepsia. The fat sluggish person is more likely to suffer from diseases of assimilation than his thin active compeer. Any one leading an out-of-door open-air life has, cæteris paribus, a better chance of escaping the deleterious effects of repletion than another who is confined to his room and his chair, and does not vitalise his blood and burn off his waste tissue by exercise and the inhalation of pure air. Among the symptoms of stomach irritation deserving special attention, we would mention chronic vomiting, or the repeated occurrence of this act, as one indicative of serious disturbance, and as likely to be the forerunner, as it is the frequent accompaniment, of organic mischief. In females it is very commonly the result of reflex influences, especially proceeding from the sexual apparatus, as in pregnancy and disturbed menstruation; but in their case, as well as in the male sex, our experience unfortunately tells us to examine into the possible abuse of alcohol, which circumstances often render it extremely difficult for the medical examiner to substantiate, though he may have strong suspicions. Where the suspicion exists the company ought certainly to have the benefit of the doubt.

Much of what has been said regarding stomach disturbance applies also to the influence exerted by the liver in determining the estimate of a patient's health. The physiological and anatomical relations of this organ render it peculiarly liable to be implicated in stomach derangement, therefore it is customary to associate stomach and liver in the inquiry suggested to the medical examiner by office forms. In cases of dyspepsia it is often difficult for the practitioner to disconnect them. It is important to remember that what we eat is of less consequence in its effect upon the liver than what we drink, owing to the immediate passage of fluids, and especially of alcoholised liquids, into the portal system. Hence this injurious influence is primarily and chiefly manifested in this organ, where they set up an irritation, which passes from simple congestion and temporary functional derangement to the various forms of severe chronic and acute disease, the effects of which every pathologist is familiar with. The previous occurrence of jaundice, habitual constipation, an enlargement of the superficial veins of the waist, especially on the right side, former hæmatemesis, frequent vomiting, a tendency to hæmorrhoids, are features in the history of the applicant that would direct special attention to the liver. Actual jaundice at the time of application would necessitate a postponement, and after its cure, which would be speedy if the cause was a catarrhal or some similar passing influence, further inquiry should be made. The habitual condition of the evacuations would assist in the conclusion, and if they had frequently exhibited a chalky or clayey appearance, the inference would be that the liver was not secreting a due quantity of bile, and, therefore, imperfectly performing its functions. We are as yet far from having attained to as correct an estimate of the variations in the hepatic secretions as we are able to form of the renal secretion, and while even the early stages of kidney disease are generally diagnosed with certainty from an examination of the urine, we constantly meet with advanced hepatic disorder either in the sick-room or in the deadhouse, where no such indication was to be found during life.

There may be a dirty sallow complexion, not amounting to actual jaundice, which indicates a sluggish performance of the hepatic duties. A congested state of the congestival vessels, a rubicund turgid nose, a full, slow, and sluggish pulse, are often associated with the same condition. Owing to the anatomical relation of the inferior hæmorrhoidal veins and the portal vein, congestion in the vessels of the rectum, as manifested in piles and the occurrence of hæmorrhage per anum, is to be regarded as evidence of inactivity of the liver, very commonly met with in intemperate people, and in others leading a sedentary life. Piles alone rarely justify rejection, but their nature and extent must be inquired into, and their condition would assist in estimating the value of other indications. Fistula in ano, in itself a curable disease, is often connected with hepatic disorder, and especially occurs in persons of a strumous habit of body, and receives importance from these circumstances.

Whether we have reason to suspect the liver or not, an examination of the hepatic region is advisable. The normal dullness of the part extends from the fifth intercostal space to the lower margin of the ribs; and any material deviation from this relation must indicate either that some external pressure is exerted upon the organ from above downwards or from below upwards, or that there is a deviation from the normal proportions in the organ itself. Emphysema of the right lung or effusion into the right pleural cavity may depress the diaphragm, and with it the liver; or fluid, or tumours in the abdominal cavity may push the liver up. Such conditions are not likely to come under the consideration of the life assurance referee; if they do, they will be readily recognised, and the effect attributed to the right cause. But if all the dimensions of the liver are altered and no such complications exist, we have to determine the nature of the enlargement. There is only one form which would not justify complete rejection, and that is enlargement depending upon simple congestion. This would necessitate the postponement of the case until the time of cure. Very considerable enlargement may be due to this cause, but as there is often a difficulty in determining the exact nature of liver enlargement, we cannot predicate the result of treatment with the same certainty that we use in many other diseases; until the liver is restored to its normal dimensions, the life is uninsurable.

The conditions that result in a reduction of the size of the liver are more difficult of recognition than those which lead to hypertrophy. The mapping out of the organ by percussion in this case is often rendered difficult by the condition of the abdominal parietes and the state of the intestines, and we shall be more generally guided to a safe conclusion by the general state and habits of the patient than by the physical examination.

The same may be said of the pancreas, the diseased conditions of which, in themselves rarely the subject of clinical observation, still more infrequently, if ever, have to be considered in reference to insurees. The total number of deaths attributed to pancreas disease (with an etc.) by the Registrar-General in 1871 is 12 for all England.

Spleen disease (etc.) claims, according to the same authority, 99 fatal cases; it is not, therefore, of much account. The spleen is frequently temporarily enlarged in fevers of various kinds; but it is only the chronic form of enlargement which commonly results from ague, a disease which, as we already had occasion to point out, is almost extinct in this country, that merits a passing observation here. The cachectic appearance of a person labouring under enlarged spleen would in itself probably suffice to cause his rejection; but an examination of the splenic region in the left hypochondrium would readily reveal any enlargement that was capable of being recognised by percussion. We should be especially on the alert in respect to this lesion in all persons, such as officers, who might have gone through malarious diseases, which are the ordinary precursors of ague-cake or permanently enlarged spleen.

It is to be feared that incipient Renal Disease is not as often recognised by the medical practitioner as the means at his disposal permit. The general symptoms at the outset are in many cases so trifling that the applicant fails to attribute them to any serious indisposition, and there may be nothing in his general appearance to draw attention to the kidneys. Hence, though the medical adviser would have no difficulty in detecting the presence of albumen or sugar in the urine were he to apply the well-known tests, he shrinks from requiring the necessary specimen for fear of appearing unnecessarily minute and pedantic. But as no medical man reports on a case for life insurance without examining the thorax, and we frequently detect mischief of which the examinee was unconscious, so no report for life insurance ought to be considered complete without a definite statement as to the condition of the urine after examination by the physician. A patient, as is well known, thinks a great deal of the turbidity and sediment due to the presence of lithates, which is of trifling import, but asserts the secretion to be healthy as long as it is clear. It is scarcely necessary to insist upon the necessity of rejection if albumen or sugar are found; unless in the former case there has been recent scarlet fever, the rejection must be absolute; but if there is scarlatinal albuminuria, the individual may be remitted to his medical attendant, to reappear when the urine is stated and found to be free from any albuminous compounds. Nor let the medical adviser be determined in advising an advanced rate because the quantity of albumen appears trifling. One of the worst forms of renal degeneration is commonly characterised by the presence of often nothing more than a trace of this abnormal adjunct.

A disorder which is not recognised by the Registrar-General as a cause of death, though it indicates serious disturbance in the assimilative process, and is frequently overlooked in private practice, is Azoturia. Characterised by the discharge of an excessive amount of urea in the urine, it is often the only tangible symptom in vague forms of gastric derangement and nervous disease. It is often troublesome to deal with, but it yields to treatment, unless, as sometimes happens, it passes into, and is interchargeable with, diabetes. If the urine exhibit a specific gravity of 1030 and upwards, and no sugar is found, an excess of urea will almost certainly prove to be the cause of the high specific gravity. The applicant should, under such circumstances, be remitted to his medical adviser, and his acceptance be postponed until he is able to present himself without blemish.

Present Hæmaturia is necessarily a disqualification. Its former occurrence would have to be estimated according to the circumstances under which it took place: if all symptoms of renal or bladder mischief had disappeared the life might be taken at the normal rates, but the causes that gave rise to the hæmaturia, unless in the case of external injury, are likely to recur; and in the case of injury there would always be the fear that, as it must have been severe to cause direct lesion of the organ, a slighter influence than would affect a healthy person would induce acute or chronic disease in the kidney.

Inflammation of the bladder, or chronic irritation of the viscus, is always to be regarded with apprehension, even if, at the time of the examination, the symptoms have passed away. Dangerous in itself, it is also a cause of renal disease. The same remark applies to stricture of the urethra, which, even if slight, should be regarded in reference to the possible more serious chronic disease of the kidneys to which it frequently gives rise later in life. The habits and mode of life of the individual may assist materially in guiding us to a right conclusion, as intemperance, anxiety, or undue exposure, might induce symptoms which under more sanitary conditions would not be likely to arise.

Among the lesions of the external parts of the body the medical adviser has to consider hernia, ulcers, skin diseases, malformations, and the effect of former injuries in maiming the individual.

Hernia, even when easily reducible, is regarded as a bar to insurance, unless the applicant consents to wear a truss, and even then it is usual to put on three years to the life. We do not think that a double hernia is in itself a cause for absolute rejection, as laid down by Dr. Allen.* Any risk resulting from a single hernia may be increased † when both sides of the body are affected, but trusses are so well made now-a-days, and the danger of neglecting their use is sufficiently impressed upon the individual, that he need not necessarily run more risk in one case than in the other. At all events a higher rate might cover it. The medical referee should, however, under all circumstances, satisfy himself that the applicant really has a hernia, as strange mistakes are sometimes made,—enlarged glands, hydroceles, tumours, and retained testes having been looked upon and treated as hernia, in which cases trusses would be more likely to do harm than good.

Open ulcers render the candidate inadmissible until they are healed, but do not occur with much frequency in the class of persons presenting themselves for insurance. Of course the presence of any syphilitic taint would affect our judgment still more

* Medical Examinations for Life Insurance, p. 44.

† A distinguished hospital surgeon whom we have consulted on this point even demurs to this conclusion, and has stated to us that he regards double hernia, cæteris paribus, as less conducive to danger than single hernia. Mr. Callender, of St. Bartholomew's Hospital, has kindly examined his own records bearing upon this question, and finds that double hernia very rarely comes under operation, and concludes that it is, therefore, seldom fatal. In 59 cases in which he operated he has only twice done so where double hernia existed.

unfavourably; and for the same reason scars of former ulcerative processes must be looked for, and their bearing upon longevity determined according to their manifest or probable causes. Scars of old scrofulous ulcers are very commonly met with, and serve as indications to the hereditary or personal proclivity of the candidate for assurance, which must not be overlooked. Among scars we would specially advert to those left by leeches, cupping, and bleeding. They are frequently forgotten until the medical man notices them; and the indications they afford as to former diseases of subjacent or adjoining viscera may assist him in prosecuting his inquiries into the past history of the individual, and open out views that the defective memory of the examinee might fail to offer.

There are scarcely any skin diseases, excepting those showing a constitutional taint, that would permanently disqualify for life insurance. If there is any doubt as to their nature, the candidate must be remitted to his own medical adviser to be cured, which would be especially the case with any secondary syphilitic eruption. Lupus or lupoid disease ought to call for a postponement of the case for the same purpose. Acne rosacea would attract special attention to the habits of the individual, and probably on this account render a higher rate desirable.

Malformations and the results of injury would have to be considered in regard to their possible interference with the functions of internal organs, and also as to whether in any way they may give rise to danger by preventing the applicant from taking the necessary care of himself in every-day life. A deaf person, or a blind person, though otherwise in perfect health, would be exposed to greater risk from accident in and out of his house than any one not subject to such defect of the special senses. Blindness is commonly charged ten years extra, but it is not customary to make an addition for deafness. The loss of a leg would induce a difficulty of locomotion, which might easily entail further accidents, while it also prevents the individual from taking the amount of exercise necessary for the preservation of health; the usual addition of three years for this defect is scarcely adequate. In all these cases special inquiry should be made as to the cause of the loss of limb or sense. Accidents rendering surgical operation necessary, and diseases followed by loss of hearing or sight, may not infrequently be traced to intemperance, to culpable carelessness, or to hereditary taint, which may influence the decision as to the rate to be fixed.

Other morbid conditions of external organs might be adverted to as disqualifying for life insurance, or necessitating high rates, but some, *e.g.*, fatty degeneration of the muscles, belong rather to the curiosities of medical experience, or bear so marked a character in abridging life, that it is unnecessary to advert to them in detail. For all exceptional cases the medical adviser must be guided by his general knowledge of medical questions, or, in case of doubt, refer to a consultant for a further opinion.

CHAPTER VIII.

THE MEDICO-LEGAL ASPECTS OF LIFE INSURANCE.

A FEW points, and among them some that especially bear upon the medico-legal aspects of life insurance, and which have not found a place in the previous chapters, remain to be considered.

It is not customary among respectable offices to underbid one another, therefore previous rejection at another insurance company militates strongly against the acceptance of a life. At the same time, it would be cruel not to take a life into consideration that proposes in proper form, and it necessarily happens not only that different views may prevail as to the importance of certain indications, but also that circumstances may have occurred since the rejection which might justify a favourable interpretation of adverse features. In many morbid conditions, time effects material improvements, and residuary affections, which once threatened danger, may have disappeared altogether, or have assumed so quiescent a form as to present no unfavourable symptoms. Thus, a person recently recovered from a pleuritic seizure might be deemed ineligible within six weeks of his illness, but after a year or more the health might and probably would be so perfectly restored as to remove all objections, unless some past indications of morbid action had arisen. Another suffering from a paralytic affection, consequent upon diphtheria, would be unacceptable while there was any trace of paralysis, but admissible when all nerve symptoms had been removed. Instances of this kind might be indefinitely multiplied.

On the other hand, previous acceptance by any office does not supersede the necessity of a strict scrutiny, when the same individual again proposes to insure. The lapse of a few years very frequently reveals new features which give the case a totally different aspect. Parents, or other relations previously in good health, may have died, and their fatal illnesses may show a taint which was not before manifest. The applicant may himself have suffered from illnesses exhibiting an hereditary predisposition that would diminish his expectation, or he may have become the subject of morbid influences affecting vital organs of a different character, equally impairing his prospect of longevity. It is so much the custom of English offices to interchange their experiences with regard to their policyholders, that a certain solidarity exists between them, and a comparison of papers and the contained statements not unfrequently exhibits discrepancies, which afford considerable assistance in estimating the value of a life. Thus, a short time since, a life was proposed to an office and reported upon by an examiner of eminence. The proposer stated that he had suffered from an attack of rheumatism. A reference to the medical attendant proved this to have been a severe attack of rheumatic fever, for which seven years extra were charged, but the proposer not agreeing to these terms, the proposal was not completed. Another equally careful office having taken the life at the tabular rates, a comparison of the papers of the two companies showed that the proposer, having ascertained the weak point in his case, had stated in his replies to the second office, that his rheumatic fever was "slight rheumatism," and that he had required no medical attendant. Applicants even unintentionally are apt to exhibit considerable obliviousness of matters connected with their own health or that of their relations; it is therefore useful to be able to remind them of statements made on a former occasion, and to compare accounts given at different periods. Wherever there is a suspicion that there has been any attempt to deceive and make a fraudulent or a highly-coloured statement, the application had better be refused altogether, as one such intentional error would necessarily more or less invalidate all other averments, and in case of future disputes, make the company a particeps criminis, if it could be shown to have connived at the fraud by knowingly accepting a life offered under false pretences.

The physician has an important interest in the medico-legal aspect of life assurance, and to estimate that fully, it may be worth while to refer briefly to what the life assurance contract realises, and in what terms the contracting parties enter into it. In all ordinary cases a person, either of his own accord or at the suggestion of others, comes to an insurance company and offers to pay an annuity or yearly sum during his life, if the company will undertake to pay his representatives a certain sum by way of reversion after his death. This being the chief condition of the contract, it remains to settle the two sums. The one, the proposer determines himself by naming the amount for which he wishes to be assured. The other, is fixed by the office on the faith of certain statements made by the proposer, and of a medical examination to which he subjects himself. This examination, however carefully or ably made, must be incomplete without the statements, comprising the age, the habits, and the personal and family history of the applicant. If these statements are not made fairly and truly, one of the contracting parties, *i.e.* the assurance company, is induced to enter into the contract in ignorance of its exact nature. Of the three subjects just mentioned, the age is capable of positive proof, and offices therefore take the statement of the age for granted, subject to subsequent evidence of its correctness, but particulars as to habits and history can only be obtained on the faith of the proposer. Some persons are under the impression that the undergoing a medical examination relieves them from the responsibility of giving false information on these points, but this is an error. One of the greatest authorities on the law of life insurance* quotes the opinion of a learned judge on the subject to the following effect:—"Not only must the party pro-

* A treatise upon the Law of Life Assurance by C. J. Bunyon, M.A., p. 30. London, 1854

posing the insurance abstain from making any deceptive representation, but he must observe the utmost degree of good faith, *uberrima fides*. Not only is he required to state all matters within his knowledge which he believes to be material to the question of the insurance, but all which in point of fact are so. If he conceals anything which he knows to be material, it is a fraud; but besides that, if he conceals anything which may influence the rate of premium, which the underwriter may require, although he does not know that it would have that effect, such concealment entirely vitiates the policy. An entire disclosure must then be made of all material facts known to the assured; and not only so, but all representations made by him as to material facts must be substantially correct; and to this may be added, that where a representation amounts to a warranty, it must not only be substantially but literally true."

For convenience, the assurance offices have adopted a form, called a declaration, on which the requisite information should be given. This form is usually annexed to the form of the medical report; and although some offices incorporate it with the report, and leave it to the medical examiner to put the questions and write down the answers as they are given by the applicant, the majority of the offices—while they annex one form to the other, thus recognising the necessity that the medical adviser should have the applicant's replies before him in order to enable him to fill up the other properly,—make the declaration a distinct document, which has to be signed by the proposer. The declaration generally has the following words, or something to the same effect, at the foot :—" I declare the above statements to be true, and admit them as the basis of my contract with the ——— company."—The questions in this declaration are generally read over to the applicant by the physician, and the former appends his signature to the answers after they are taken down.

The modern custom appears to be to put a distinct question as to each important disease of ordinary occurrence, and the questions doubtless appear to the inexperienced to be unnecessarily numerous. But this is quite as much in the interest of the proposer as of the office, and to prevent the former from forgetting any fact that ought to be mentioned. At the same time the responsibility of giving full information rests with the proposer, as laid down in the quotation previously given from Mr. Bunyon's work. He subsequently * adds the following authoritative statement :—" If the proposer leads the insurers into error, by inducing them to compute their risk upon circumstances not founded in fact, so that the risk actually run is different to that intended to be run, the contract is as much at an end as if there had been a wilful and false allegation, or an undue concealment of circumstances."

This being the law, it appears to be the duty of the medical examiner to protect both the proposer and the office from the results of its being broken. In practice, offices rarely dispute the payment of a

* *Loco citato*, p. 33.

policy unless fraud of a most glaring and deliberate kind has been committed; but it cannot be doubted that frauds are practised upon them; and that by the withholding or misstatment of certain facts, directors are frequently led to pass lives at the ordinary rate, when they ought to have been charged an extra premium. Take a case like the one previously alluded to, where a proposer had been affected with rheumatic fever, and who states he had only had a slight attack of rheumatism. The former, assuming the proposer's age to be 30, would necessitate an extra charge of seven years, while the latter would not render an addition necessary. The fraud here consists in the value of the difference in the premiums, or in an assurance for £1000 (say Carlisle 4 per cent) = £78 : 6s. Or, in the case of a man whose mother died of consumption, but who states that she died after childbirth, there ought to be an addition of 10 years; and if, in consequence of his false statement, he is taken at the ordinary rates, the office is defrauded of £125 : 12s.

Hence it should be the duty of the medical man to impress upon the proposer the necessity of truth and exactness, and to cross-examine him on any point on which he fails to reply frankly and satisfactorily. Some people think it no harm to benefit themselves at the expense of a public company, but by the prevailing constitution of assurance societies, by which a large majority of the policyholders are assured on the system of participating in the profits, the injury done affects the members, and each one bears his proportion of it.

Another point in connection with the subject under consideration is the relation of the private medical attendant. One of the questions addressed to a proposer is: Who is your ordinary medical attendant? and many controversies have arisen on the answer given. It is clear there is room for serious fraud here, as experience has shown. It is the custom in one London office always to constitute the private medical attendant its own examiner pro tempore, and to give an additional fee in consequence. The definition of what constitutes a private medical attendant is given in the papers of the office in question, thus:—The medical man who has most frequently attended the life proposed.

Life assurance now being widely diffused over the country, this plan would be practically adopted by many offices, for in small towns and villages it must often happen that the medical examiner is also the medical attendant of the proposer. But in populous towns and districts this is less likely to happen, and we are then driven back to the question. The reply would necessarily yield the name of the practitioner who could give the most complete information regarding the proposer. It might happen that a candidate for insurance had been attended by one medical man for a dangerous illness most prejudicial to longevity, and soon after by another for some trifling ailment. To name the latter as the ordinary medical attendant might be a compliance with the query in its literal sense, but certainly not with its spirit. In the case of *Everett* versus *Desborough*,* it was laid down that a refer-

* Bunyon, *loc. cit.* p. 44.

ence to a person who immediately before the time at which the policy is effected has been casually consulted for trifling maladies, will not satisfy the requisition for a reference to the usual medical attendant, although the person who had formerly attended may have retired from practice at the time.

We cannot put the matter in a clearer and more succinct form than by laying before our readers the following further extract from Mr. Bunyon's work; which seems to comprise all the legal bearings of the subject:—

"The meaning of the question 'Who is your usual medical attendant?' was elaborately considered in the case lastly referred to (*Everett* v. *Desborough*).

'What is the grammatical sense of that question?' observed the court: 'It is in the present tense.' Suppose a person goes to effect a policy on his life, who had no medical attendant in the last year; if the answer to the question were, 'I have no such medical attendant,' must not that question of necessity be followed by another, which is, 'Who was your former medical attendant?' The terms and nature of the question prove that it was designed to extract from the person *who is the medical attendant best able to give an account of her constitution at the time;* and if she has no usual medical attendant in the precise grammatical sense of the question, it appears to me that she is bound to mention who is the medical attendant who could give that information. The facts of the case appear to be, that this lady had been attended by Mr. Duck, her medical man at Bristol, for a considerable time during several years, and down to the time of her marriage in December 1832. Previously to her marriage she had made one or two attempts to effect a policy on her life, and Mr. Duck had been referred to as her medical attendant, and on his representations the parties with whom it was proposed to effect the insurance had declined the risk. She was married in December 1832, and it was stated that from that time Mr. Duck ceased to attend her, but that a gentleman of the name of Day, who had been attending her husband, and was the usual medical attendant of the family, upon one or two occasions, not being called in to attend her expressly, but incidentally calling, had given her some slight advice of such little note that he had made no memorandum of it in his book. When called upon to answer the question, she replied, 'Mr. Day,' who being examined by the company's agent, said she was perfectly well for aught he knew, and that he had never attended her professionally at all; and on trial, that he had attended her once or twice: he was not sure that he had attended her a second time, but he had once or twice given advice to her. The question was left to the jury to say whether Mr. Duck or Mr. Day was her usual medical attendant; but it appears to the Court that there was another question behind, namely, whether, from the peculiar circumstances under which Mr. Day was introduced to her notice, he could be called her usual medical attendant at all. It appears to us that it should have been laid down to the jury, that, if she was aware that the person whose name she gave could not be the proper person to render the account that the defendant wished to have of her, it was her duty to have mentioned the circumstance, and to have stated that although Mr. Day was a person to whom they might refer, he was not the usual medical attendant, but that the usual attendant had been Mr. Duck. To illustrate this, suppose Mr. Day had never attended her at all, but that when she married she ceased to have any medical attendant; suppose she had answered, 'I have no usual medical attendant,' that answer would have been followed by the question, 'But had you ever any usual medical attendant?' She must have known that the question was intended to elicit from her an answer designating the person who could give the best information respecting the state of her constitution."

It is well known that for a long time a controversy was carried on between the life offices and the medical profession on the subject of medical fees. It was urged by the former that a proposer for an assurance was bound, as a person selling a property, to prove his title at his own cost, but that the company had the right to make all needful requisitions. On the other hand, it was argued that if so, the medical man, being in the pay and interest of the proposer, was rather his advocate. This contest has now ended. The offices admit that the medical man, if asked to report, does so in their interest, and should be paid by them. It has been suggested that the sympathies of the private medical attendant are on the side of his patient, but practically, if this is the case, it is not found to warp his judgment and to induce the return of false statements. If he allowed his feelings or prejudices to guide him, it is the more necessary that he should be acquainted with the clear injunctions of the law as to his duties, which are calculated to induce him to be perfectly frank, and to make a full statement of everything within his knowledge that is at all likely to affect what is termed the basis of the contract of life assurance. Anything like reservation clearly jeopardises the entire transaction, and places the policy-holder at the mercy of the company.

The medical officer of an insurance company has an important office to fulfil in examining the claim papers; he has to satisfy himself of the nature of the evidence of death, and he ought especially to inquire into the causes of the fatal issue. In doing this he would have three objects in view: first, to ascertain that the death is attributable to natural causes; second, to determine whether there is any discrepancy between the statements of the late policyholder, regarding his health and the fatal disease; and third, to extract from each individual case any information that may avail him in judging of future lives to be submitted to his judgment.

A death from natural causes excludes the idea of suicide, which almost universally invalidates a policy, though for our part we are strongly of opinion that unless suicide is committed within a certain space of time from the date of the first issue of the policy, it ought to be regarded like any other accident, to be provided for by the rates of insurance.

The number of suicides in England in 1871 was 1495, of which 1103 were males and 392 females — the average for London alone from 1846-1850 was about 240 annually, of which less than half were females. The proportions manifestly vary somewhat in town and country; the total number for London in 1871 was 207; therefore, considering the vast increase of the population during the last 25 years, this looks like improvement. Suicides occur chiefly in the middle and upper ranks of society, whose position and property fluctuate much more, involving greater anxiety and mental distress than is the case among working classes; hence, although the proportion to the entire population is small, the proportion falling upon insurance companies, which are chiefly resorted to by the former, is comparatively large. This is further corroborated by the table quoted from Mr. Smee junior, at page 117, where the deaths from violence, which includes suicides, are found to constitute a high ratio, though this of course is imperfect evidence, as we have not the numbers of deaths from other causes included under the head of violence. Judging by the evidence at our disposal, it appears that 5 claims in 1000 are due to suicide. Suicide is a direct result of what is termed civilisation. The proportion which it bears to the population exhibits a close ratio to the advance of education and wealth. It is generally larger in towns than in the country. Casper,* the great German medico-

* Quoted by Quetelet, Sur l'Homme, vol. ii. p. 147. See also two valuable papers on Suicide, by Mr. Jopling, in the Assurance Magazine, vols. i. and ii.

legal authority, gives the following table as the result of his inquiries into the frequency of suicides in certain towns of importance :—

	Number of suicides to 100,000 inhabitants.	One suicide to number of inhabitants.
Copenhagen	100	1000
Paris	49	2040
Hamburg	45	2222
Berlin	34	2941
London	20	5000
Elberfeld	20	5000

Quetelet also gives the authority of his imprimatur to the following quotation from Balbi,* which the reader may like to refer to as bearing upon the general social aspect of suicide. The data appear to have been collected in or about 1827. The number of suicides were in

Russia, in the proportion of	1 to 49,182	inhabitants.
Austrian Empire	,, 20,900	,,
France ,,	,, 20,740	,,
Philadelphia ,,	,, 15,875	,,
Prussia ,,	,, 14,404	,,
Baltimore ,,	,, 13,656	,,
Boston ,,	,, 12,500	,,
New York ,,	,, 7,797	,,

To the list of the sad sequelæ to intemperance we have also to add suicide, with which it is too often found associated. Dr. Farr has shown that the professions peculiarly addicted to drunkenness have more than their due proportion of suicides. "Drunkenness," he says, "leads to this, but drunkenness is a sort of in-

* "La Monarchie Française comparée aux principaux états du globe."

direct suicide, and both are tendencies of the mind indulged often from the same motives, and promoted by similar causes; for in drunkenness the wretched find not only the gratification of an appetite, but the suspension of natural consciousness—in death they seek its cessation."

To pass from these general statistics to the consideration of the subject immediately before us, it may be stated that it is not always easy to determine whether an individual has died by his own voluntary act or not; and as insurance companies shrink from contesting their liability, although under their contract fully empowered to do so under certain conditions, owing to the odium which they incur, unless they are certain of being able to prove the correctness of their suspicions, it is tolerably certain that a considerable number of claims have been paid although life had been terminated by suicide. A claim of this kind lately came before us, where morally there could scarcely be any doubt that a captain, who, without adequate motive, not only refused to leave his sinking ship after his mate and all the sailors had taken to their boats, but even lay down in his berth, and declined urgent solicitations to escape from certain death, was guilty of suicide; yet the company consented to pay the policy, owing to the conviction that a jury would certainly have looked upon him as a martyr and a hero. Most persons of any experience in these matters will probably recall more marked illustrations of this feature in life insurance.

However, we repeat that we would not even allow

well-proven suicide to invalidate a policy after a lapse of say five years, because it is not to be supposed that any one would take out a policy with the view of defrauding the company so long beforehand, because it is generally desirable to fix a time at which all policies become absolutely indisputable, and because there is sufficient evidence to justify the belief that suicide is generally the consequence of a morbid condition of the body or the mind, or both. If all insurance companies agreed to adopt some principle of the kind, and resolutely acted upon it, the temptation to this species of fraud would be removed, and the poor survivors would not lose what in these cases is often their only stay.

A certain amount of sympathy cannot be denied to persons, who, with the intention of benefiting *those dear to them, make away with themselves.* The moral obliquity which is associated with suicide is often to be interpreted as a perversion of one of our best feelings; and the individual who commits the act doubtless thinks at times that he is committing an act of self-sacrifice for the good of others. The anxiety and distress which commonly lead to self-destruction are generally an efficient cause in overthrowing the balance of the mind, and if we cannot agree with the almost universal verdict of juries, that "temporary insanity" palliated the deed; neither can we doubt that before a higher tribunal an intimate knowledge of the physical and moral circumstances surrounding the case would, in many cases, conduce to a verdict that it belonged rather to the category of disease than of crime.

But if a sentiment of pity softens the asperity of our feelings with regard to the individual who defrauds the insurance company by taking away his own life, no expression of condemnation can be too strong to apply to those who, for the sake of this species of gain, contemplate and carry out the destruction of others. Unfortunately, our records exhibit many instances of this form of crime; wives, parents, brothers, friends, have been insured and murdered for the sake of the proceeds of the policy. In the lower ranks of life, burial clubs have been repeatedly shown to act as incentives to crime of the same kind. All through society, therefore, it behoves the medical man to be on his guard, that he may detect any indication of a life having been tampered with. In this respect he cannot refuse to watch over public morality; and in connection with life insurance, he has the further motive, if any be required, that other important interests are committed to his charge, and that the discovery of this form of crime rests especially with him.

In conclusion, we would express a hope that we have conveyed to our medical readers, throughout, the high moral responsibilities which they incur in undertaking the work which legitimately pertains to them in connection with life insurance. Although we have had occasion to advert to the possibility of shortcomings in members of the medical profession, our general experience, now of many years' duration, of the work done by them, justifies the assertion, that as a rule they act upon the principle enunciated in the passage which Shakspeare puts into the mouth of one of his chief characters:

> "Tis not my profit that does lead mine honour;
> Mine honour, it."

Life insurance involves interests of the greatest importance to the individual and to society; and here as in many other matters affecting the welfare of humanity, the medical man is one of the chief guardians of social morality and civilisation. The more fully he realises the elevated aims that he should aspire to, the more he aids his fellow-man in his onward progress, and the more he fulfils the great obligations which he takes upon himself in joining the noblest and the most unselfish of all professions.

APPENDIX.

Causes of Death.	1852	1853	1854	1855	1856	1857	1858	1859
All causes	407,135	421,097	437,905	425,703	390,506	419,815	449,656	440,781
Specified causes . .	394,357	407,752	425,645	413,359	379,828	409,719	440,922	432,476
CLASSES.								
1. Zymotic Diseases . .	96,233	89,564	117,135	88,383	81,375	93,634	110,971	106,645
2. Constitutional . .	83,035	88,216	83,993	84,645	79,500	81,969	82,416	81,788
3. Local	135,415	147,138	143,481	156,953	142,761	151,531	163,489	159,686
4. Developmental . .	66,154	69,105	66,996	69,253	62,232	68,668	69,895	69,708
5. Violent Deaths . .	13,520	13,729	14,040	14,125	13,960	13,917	14,151	14,649
ORDERS.								
1.								
1. Miasmatic Diseases .	92,305	85,515	112,612	83,726	77,270	89,296	106,278	101,699
2. Enthetic . . .	889	874	1,236	1,190	1,069	1,147	1,195	1,273
3. Dietic	1,676	1,857	1,980	2,087	1,688	1,905	2,112	2,301
4. Parasitic . . .	1,363	1,318	1,307	1,380	1,348	1,286	1,386	1,372
2.								
1. Diathetic . . .	16,872	17,601	16,848	17,125	15,668	16,207	16,790	16,433
2. Tubercular . . .	66,163	70,615	67,145	67,520	63,832	65,762	65,626	65,355
3.								
1. Diseases of Nervous System . . .	50,246	51,509	51,485	52,365	50,084	51,619	53,961	54,531
2. Organs of Circulation .	12,517	13,740	13,488	14,573	13,691	14,802	16,426	17,133
3. Respiratory Organs .	47,400	56,436	52,484	63,820	52,973	58,378	65,516	59,853
4. Digestive Organs . .	18,905	18,749	18,885	18,885	18,710	19,360	19,246	19,842
5. Urinary Organs . .	3,438	3,652	3,770	4,042	4,227	4,202	4,683	4,736
6. Organs of Generation .	877	960	1,014	1,042	1,039	1,069	1,148	1,199
7. Organs of Locomotion .	1,139	1,227	1,500	1,428	1,329	1,306	1,164	1,285
8. Integumentary System	893	865	855	798	708	795	1,345	1,107
4.								
1. Developmental Diseases of Children . .	12,292	12,541	12,541	12,081	11,586	12,617	12,412	12,300
2. Adults	2,373	2,383	2,125	2,024	1,932	2,042	2,114	2,314
3. Old People . . .	26,376	29,130	26,466	29,714	23,931	26,847	28,509	27,104
4. Diseases of Nutrition .	25,113	25,051	25,864	25,434	24,783	27,162	26,860	27,990
5.								
1. Accident or Negligence }	13,520	13,729	14,040	14,125	13,960	13,917	12,523	13,056
2. Battle . . . }								
3. Homicide . . }							344	338
4. Suicide . . . }							1,275	1,248
5. Execution * . . }							9	7
Violent deaths not classed }								
Sudden deaths, cause unascertained . .	3,591	4,018	3,993	4,139	3,474	3,403	3,096	2,821
Causes not specified .	9,187	9,327	8,267	8,205	7,204	6,693	5,638	5,484

* The number of persons executed in the several years will not necessarily correspond with that are classed in the latter according to the dates of conviction, while the num-

.860	1861	1862	1863	1864	1865	1866	1867	1868	1869	1870	1871
22,721	435,114	436,566	473,837	495,531	490,909	500,689	471,073	480,622	494,828	515,329	514,879
14,060	427,360	429,000	465,874	487,732	482,509	492,111	462,939	473,773	488,117	507,921	507,713
75,849	87,986	91,539	119,731	118,825	113,948	115,972	90,989	117,356	110,601	120,511	123,030
82,088	84,987	83,024	84,393	87,190	85,504	89,907	89,423	85,340	86,730	88,766	87,072
71,037	167,454	170,651	174,603	189,039	184,877	192,444	187,571	178,634	199,976	205,264	204,362
70,311	71,948	68,842	71,467	75,660	77,806	76,873	78,090	75,475	74,313	76,787	76,256
14,775	14,985	14,944	15,680	17,018	17,374	16,915	16,866	16,968	16,497	16,593	16,993
71,304	83,324	86,881	114,538	113,051	107,650	110,059	84,985	111,106	104,670	114,468	117,093
1,252	1,355	1,449	1,578	1,793	1,914	1,893	1,909	2,101	2,108	2,084	2,056
2,206	2,095	2,149	2,456	2,810	2,957	2,888	2,760	2,853	2,645	2,605	2,602
1,087	1,212	1,060	1,159	1,171	1,427	1,132	1,335	1,296	1,178	1,354	1,279
16,404	16,233	16,412	16,651	17,392	17,437	17,482	17,520	17,039	17,511	17,481	17,061
65,684	68,754	66,612	67,742	69,798	71,067	72,425	71,903	68,301	69,219	71,285	70,011
55,577	56,625	55,692	57,428	59,627	60,264	61,164	60,367	60,174	61,550	63,856	62,453
18,758	18,076	18,709	19,505	22,419	22,272	22,190	22,784	22,558	24,899	25,259	26,219
68,408	64,310	67,565	67,280	75,376	69,952	77,249	72,183	63,103	80,397	82,186	81,825
19,718	20,327	19,421	20,516	20,969	21,774	21,084	21,006	21,479	21,315	21,853	21,621
4,990	5,222	5,328	5,578	6,104	6,274	6,621	6,933	6,872	7,319	7,503	7,628
1,118	1,129	1,227	1,219	1,294	1,241	1,241	1,316	1,258	1,283	1,298	1,221
1,466	1,624	1,588	1,765	1,860	1,860	1.642	1,747	1,833	1,846	1,893	1,997
1,002	1,141	1,121	1,312	1,390	1,240	1,253	1,235	1,357	1,367	1,416	1,398
12,706	13,116	12,787	13,498	13,921	14,360	14,634	14,666	14,334	14,203	14,858	15,176
2,233	2,168	2,198	2,508	2,607	2,576	2,596	2,461	2,437	2,224	2,510	2,584
28,442	27,373	26,780	27,268	29,498	28,709	28,546	28,646	26,050	27,932	28,889	28,038
26,930	29,291	27,077	28,193	29,634	32,161	31,097	32,317	32,654	29,954	30,530	30,458
12,991	13,187	13,055	13,772	15,091	15,232	14,886	14,848	14,715	14,260	14,393	14,961
377	320	418	399	412	443	480	392	461	387	381	381
1,365	1,347	1,317	1,319	1,340	1,392	1,329	1,316	1,508	1,588	1,554	1,495
10	11	17	21	21	6	12	11	10	8	7	4
32	120	137	169	154	301	208	299	274	254	258	152
2,894	2,697	2,778	3,008	3,321	3,173	3,585	3,506	2,945	3,040	3,180	3,155
5,767	5,057	4,788	4,955	4,478	5,227	4,993	4,628	3,904	3,671	4,228	4,011

in the same years of the "Criminal Returns," inasmuch as the executions recorded in each year
bers in this Table are placed in the years in which the deaths are registered.

INDEX.

www.ingramcontent.com/pod-product-compliance
Lightning Source LLC
LaVergne TN
LVHW011226110826
845150LV00006B/1563

9781425516031